THEMATIC UNIT
PENGUINS

Written by Lola Willrich
Illustrated by Sue Fullam and Keith Vasconcelles

Teacher Created Materials, Inc.
6421 Industry Way
Westminster, CA 92683
www.teachercreated.com

©1991 Teacher Created Materials, Inc.
Reprinted, 2002
Made in U.S.A.
ISBN 1-55734-277-6

Table of Contents

Introduction

Penguins contains a captivating, whole language, thematic unit. Its 80 exciting, reproducible pages are filled with a wide variety of lesson ideas and activities designed for use with primary children. At its core are two high-quality children's literature selections, *The Penguin* and *Mr. Popper's Penguins*. For these books, activities are included which set the stage for reading, encourage the enjoyment of the book, and extend the concepts gained. In addition, the theme is connected to the curriculum with activities in language arts (including daily writing suggestions), math, science, social studies, art, music, and life skills (cooking, physical education, career awareness etc.). Many of these activities encourage cooperative learning. Suggestions and patterns for bulletin boards and unit management tools are additional time savers for the busy teacher. Furthermore, directions are given for student-created Big Books and a culminating activity, which allow students to synthesize their knowledge in order to produce products that can be shared beyond the classroom.

This thematic unit includes:

❏ literature selections—summaries of two children's books with related lessons (complete with reproducible pages) that cross the curriculum

❏ **poetry**—suggested selections and lessons enabling students to write and publish their own works

❏ planning guides—suggestions for sequencing lessons each day of the unit

❏ writing ideas—daily suggestions as well as writing activities across the curriculum, including Big Books

❏ bulletin board ideas—suggestions and plans for student-created and/or interactive bulletin boards

❏ homework suggestions—extending the unit to the child's home

❏ **curriculum connections** — in language arts, math, science, social studies, art, music, and life skills such as cooking, physical education, and career awareness

❏ **group projects**—to foster cooperative learning

❏ **a culminating activity**—which requires students to synthesize their learning to produce a product or engage in an activity that can be shared with others

❏ **a bibliography**—suggesting additional literature and nonfiction books on the theme

---

To keep this valuable resource Intact so that it can be used year after year, you may wish to punch holes In the pages and store them In a three-ring binder.

Introduction *(cont.)*

Why Whole Language

A whole language approach involves children in using all modes of communication: reading, writing, listening, observing, illustrating, experiencing, and doing. Communication skills are interconnected and integrated into lessons that emphasize the whole of language rather than isolating its parts. The lessons revolve around selected literature. Reading is not taught as a separate subject from writing and spelling, for example. A child reads, writes (spelling appropriately for his/her level), speaks, listens, etc. in response to a literature experience introduced by the teacher. In this way, language skills grow naturally, stimulated by involvement and interest in the topic at hand.

Why Thematic Planning?

One very useful tool for implementing an integrated whole language program is thematic planning. By choosing a theme with correlating literature selections for a unit of study, a teacher can plan activities throughout the day that lead to a cohesive, in-depth study of the topic. Students will be practicing and applying their skills in meaningful contexts. Consequently, they tend to learn and retain more. Both teachers and students will be freed from a day that is broken into unrelated segments of isolated drill and practice.

Why Cooperative Learning?

Besides academic skills and content, students need to learn social skills. No longer can this area of development be taken for granted. Students must learn to work cooperatively in groups in order to function well in modern society. Group activities should be a regular part of school life and teachers should consciously include social objectives as well as academic objectives in their planning. For example, a group working together to write a report may need to select a leader. The teacher should make clear to the students and monitor the qualities of good leader-follower group interaction just as he/she would state and monitor the academic goals of the project.

Why Big Books

An excellent cooperative, whole language activity is the production of Big Books. Groups of students, or the whole class, can apply their language skills, content knowledge, and creativity to produce a Big Book that can become a part of the classroom library to be read and reread. These books make excellent culminating projects for sharing beyond the classroom with parents, librarians, other classes, etc. Big Books can be produced in many ways and this thematic unit book includes directions for at least one method you may choose.

The Penguin Animal Close Ups

by Beatrice Fontanel

Summary

This non-fiction book details the lives of members of the King penguin family. The beautiful pictures complement the presentation of facts about the penguin's habitat, mating, life of a chick, and survival in the severe winters of Antarctica. The text follows the life of the King penguins through the calendar year, beginning in the summer month of November, when the penguins leave the ocean to find a mate. During January, the chicks hatch and then are fed and protected by both the mother and father penguins. As winter begins in May, the parent penguins leave the babies in colonies to go fishing for food.

Sample Plan

Day I

- Prepare for unit (page 6)
- Read *The Penguin*
- Start calendar activities (page 8)
- Record daily temperature; compare it to average South Pole temperatures
- Begin vocabulary activities (page 10)
- True or False? (page 56)

Day II

- Calendar activity (page 8)
- Calendar activity (page 8)
- Reread *The Penguin*
- Science: Thermometers (page 57)
- Fingerplay (page 19)
- Math: Snack Attack (page 50)
- Nutrition: Make a seafood snack (page 71) and do a Food Pyramid (page 70)
- Use Questions? Questions? Questions? (page 9)
- Do following directions activity (page 47)
- Do chant activity (#7, page 42)

Day 3

- Review *The Penguin* for sequence
- Make A Seasonal Time Line (page 14)
- Calendar activity (page 8)

- Penguin Poems worksheets (pages 35-36)
- The Nest the Penguin Built (page 13)
- Partner Word Search (page 12)
- Categorizing Animals (#6, page 41)

Day 4

- Study emperor penguins
- Compare emperor and King penguins (page 15)
- Calendar activity (page 8)
- Map activity (page 59)
- Writing Penguin Poetry (page 37)
- Animal Babies (#l, page 7)
- Begin homonym bulletin board (#8, page 42)
- Homework: List of homonyms

Day 5

- Calendar activity (page 8)
- Readers' Theater (pages 17-18)
- Drawing Conclusions (page 16)
- Vocabulary Bingo (page 46)
- Begin Penguin Number Book (page 49)
- Make and demonstrate Take Home Game (pages 20-21)

Overview of Activities

SETTING THE STAGE

1. The day before you prepare your classroom for the penguin unit hold up sheets of black and white paper. Tell students the papers are a clue to the animals you will be studying next. Have them make some guesses. When penguins have been suggested, ask them to tell you anything they know about them. List the suggestions on chart paper. Take all suggestions but indicate that revisions may be needed as learning progresses.

2. Prepare your classroom for the penguin unit by creating the bulletin board suggested on page 42 and setting up appropriate learning centers. Whenever possible, have students work in pairs to complete the center projects. Duplicate the penguin, page 77, and post it at each center. Ask students to sign their names and the date in one of the squares when they have completed the center work. The following activities may be used at centers: Punctuation Penguins (page 44), Let's Talk Penguin (page 68), Money Matters (page 52), Posting Vowels to Penguins (page 48), and A Balanced Menu (page 70).

3. List the characteristics of each of the four seasons using webs. Include the months found in each season. Explain the seasons in the Southern Hemisphere where penguins live are reversed from those in the Northern Hemisphere. List the months in each season at the South Pole (see page 14).

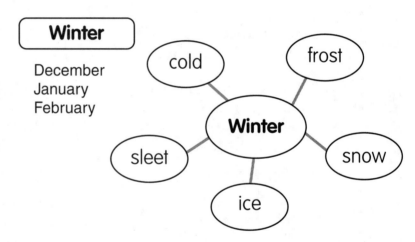

4. Locate Antarctica on a map and globe. Locate your home. After discussion of the differences in climate, have students complete the map activity on page 59.

ENJOYING THE BOOK

1. Read *The Penguin* aloud. Emphasize the months and seasons as they are mentioned in the story. Discuss the differences among species of penguins as reported on page 26 and 27 of the book.

2. Reproduce copies of the calendar on page 8 for each child. Glue them to the outside of large manila envelopes. Do an activity from the calendar each day; circle completed assignments. Keep dated activities inside the envelope. Collect a few envelopes each day for assessment.

3. Use Questions? Questions? Questions? (page 9) after reading *The Penguin*. This activity can be repeated several times throughout the unit in relationship to any facts or literature studied.

4. Begin a Penguin Word Bank chart. (For directions, see page 10.) Follow up by using the vocabulary activities on pages 10-12 and throughout the unit.

Overview of Activities *(cont.)*

ENJOYING THE BOOK *(cont.)*

5. Put the following chart on a wall or closet door. Fill in the spaces as a group or let children work on it as a free time activity.

P	**E**	**N**	**G**	**U**	**I**	**N**	**S**
Book Titles	Peter's Chair		Noah's Ark		Ira sleeps over		
Animals							
Vegetables	peas						spinach
Countries		England		Uruguay			
Birds	penguin's		gold-finch				swallow

6. Place two large penguin shapes on the wall. (You may wish to enlarge the pattern on page 39.) On the white stomachs write " Penguins can . . ." and " Penguins are . . ." Have students suggest and write words to finish the two sentences as the unit progresses.

7. Name other animals that hatch from eggs. Share a Big Book, *Hatched From an Egg* by JoAnne Nelson (Modern Curriculum Press, Young Explorer Series) or *Chickens Aren't the Only Ones* by Ruth Heller (Scholastic Big Books), to spark discussion.

EXTENDING THE BOOK

1. Make a Big Book of animals and their babies.

2. Read several animal poems from Eric Carle's *Animals, Animals* and categorize the animals (#6, page 41).

3. Take turns doing the Readers' Theater (pages 17 and 18). Or, for younger students use the Fingerplay activities on page 19.

4. Duplicate the Take Home Game for students (pages 20 and 21).

5. Penguins eat fish; so do we. Try eating some fish. Make a seafood treat (recipes, page 71). Eating fish is good, but aren't we glad our diets also include meats, vegetables, fruits, breads, cereals, and dairy products? Use A Balanced Menu, page 70.

6. Fill a sturdy nylon backpack with paper, markers, pencils, crayons and a couple of good penguin stories. Send the backpack home with a different student each night. Include a note to parents asking them to read the books to their child and help him/her create and illustrate a penguin story or poem to share with the class. (Half the fun of writing is sharing so provide an "author chair" and allow four or five students to share each day. Encourage the other students to be good listeners and give the "authors" positive comments about their work.) These writings may be made into penguin shape books to place in local doctor or dentist offices. Public libraries also like to display children's books. Use the pattern on page 39 as a cover and trace its outline for pages.

7. Make a frosty black and white penguin. See directions, page 69.

9. Make a watercolor wash art project. See directions, page 69.

Penguin Calendar

Month _____

Sunday	Monday	Tuesday	Wednesday	Thursday	Friday	Saturday
	List 5 things that are always white.	List 5 things that are always black.	List 5 animals with names beginning with "p".	List 5 animals that live in the sea.	List 5 animals that lay eggs.	
	List 5 animals with feathers.	List 5 kinds of fish. Which kind do you like to eat?	List 5 reasons why you would like to live in Antarctica.	List the 7 continents.	What is your favorite season? Tell why in 3 sentences.	
	Write 3 sentences that are true about penguins.	List 5 animals with short tails.	List 5 reasons why you would not like to live in Antarctica.	Penguins swim, waddle, and slide. List 5 ways you can move.	Write 5 "wh" sentences about penguins. (who, what, when, where, why)	
	Look on the map for names of 4 oceans. List them.	List 5 words that rhyme with "snow".	Write the titles and authors of 3 penguin books.	List the 4 seasons. Write something nice about each one.	Write an ad trying to sell your pet penguin.	
	List 5 words that rhyme with "ice".	Write the names of your state. Write the names of 4 states near you.	List 5 flavors of ice cream. Underline your favorite.	List 5 foods that begin with the letter "p".	Beginning with January, list all 12 months.	

Note to Teacher: Students add name of month and date. Activities on unnumbered spaces may be extra-credit assignments.

Questions? Questions? Questions?

Write five "WH" questions (on a topic assigned by your teacher) to exchange with a classmate. Your classmate will answer your questions in complete sentences and return them to you for checking.

Who _____

_____

_____

What _____

_____

_____

When _____

_____

_____

Where _____

_____

_____

Why _____

_____

_____

Vocabulary Activities

Penguin Word Bank Chart

Post a large penguin shape in your classroom. You may enlarge the pattern (minus the dotted lines) from page 11. Record the vocabulary learned during the unit on the penguin's stomach. Numbering the words as you add them to the list will make using the chart easier.

Here are some words to get your list started:

waddle	flippers	tuxedos	dolphin	Adélie	emperor
cooperate	penguin	colony	beaks	chick	molting
Antarctica	survival	waterproof	ocean	South Pole	species
webbed feet	feathers	elephant seal	insulating fat	penguin	winter
Antarctic Ocean	cold	Southern Hemisphere	skua gull	ice	

Using the Chart

1. When students are writing during the unit, refer to words from the chart by number when they ask for ideas or spellings.

2. Ask someone to read the odd-numbered or even-numbered words aloud whenever there is an extra minute.

3. Use the words for language activities. For example:

   • Have someone use word #3 in an asking sentence and word #5 in a telling sentence. Think of a rhyming word for #10.

   • Alphabetize the list.

   • Pick out all of the words with long "o" vowels or two syllables or plural endings, etc.

4. Make word games using the chart. See page 12 for an example.

Penguin Review Strip

Copy the penguin pattern on page 11 onto heavy paper. Cut out. Cut on the dotted lines. Prepare an oaktag strip three inches wide by 12-14 inches (7.5 X 30-35 cm) long. Divide it into one inch (2.5 cm) sections and write vocabulary words in each section except the top and bottom ones. Insert the strip into the slits on the penguin so that vocabulary words are exposed. Fold the top and bottom sections of the strip down to keep it from falling out. Students may want to work in pairs to "slide" through the vocabulary words!

Variation: Adapt the penguin pattern for math fact review by cutting out the marked section between the two slits. Write math facts in the sections of the strip. Insert into penguin. As each fact slides into view, write the answer in the opening on the back to make it self-checking. (See diagrams on page 11.)

Penguin Pattern

• See directions for Penguin Review Strip on page 10.

penguin

4+3=

2
8
10
5
⑦
4
9
3
1

Partner Word Search

1. Write nine words from the Penguin Word Bank Chart in your classroom on the lines below.

2. Put them horizontally, vertically, or diagonally in the graph squares.

3. Fill In the remaining squares with random letters.

4. Exchange papers with a partner and search.

_____   _____   _____

_____   _____   _____

_____   _____   _____

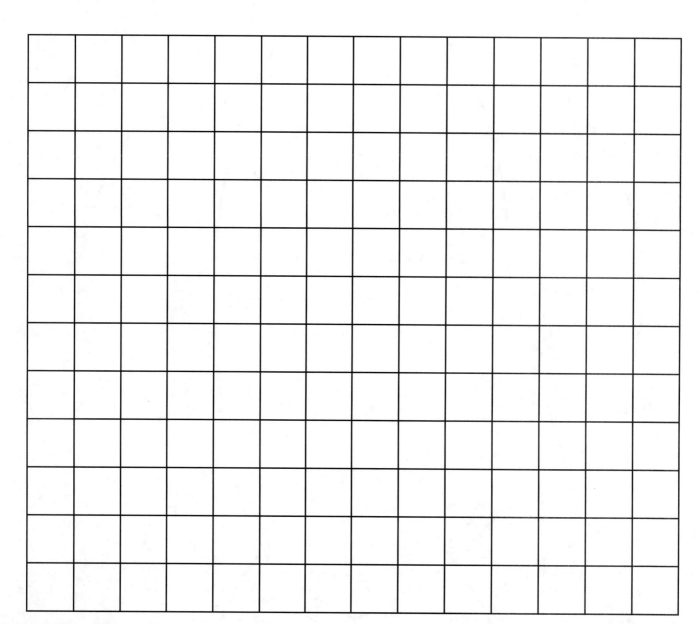

The Nest the Penguin Built

Read "The House That Jack Built." (One version can be found in *Childcraft*, Vol. 1, pp. 58-59, World Book, Inc., 1987 edition.) Then read this penguin version.

This is the nest that the penguin built.

This is the egg
That lay in the nest that the penguin built.

This is the rookery,
That protects the egg
That lay in the nest that the penguin built.

This is the chick,
That was born in the rookery,
That protects the egg
That lay in the nest that the penguin built.

This is the fish,
That was eaten by the chick,
That was born in the rookery,
That protects the egg
That lay in the nest that the penguin built.

This is the sea,
That was the home of the fish,
That was eaten by the chick,
That was born in the rookery,
That protects the egg
That lay in the nest that the penguin built.

This is the seal,
That waits in the sea,
That was the home of the fish,
That was eaten by the chick,
That was born in the rookery,
That protects the egg
That lay in the nest that the penguin built.

This is the feather,
From the mouth of the seal,
That waits in the sea,
That was the home of the fish,
That was eaten by the chick,
That was born in the rookery,
That protects the egg
That lay in the nest that the penguin built.

Swim fast, penguins!

Using the Poem

1. Make a class Big Book. (You may use the variation given here or write a new one with your class.) The stanzas may be written on large sheets of paper and small groups assigned to illustrate them. Assemble and bind with tape, rings, or yarn.

2. Use the poem as a choral reading. Assign each phrase to a child or small group of children. Whenever the phrase appears, this child or group will read it. Everyone will read the last line together.

Seasonal Time Line

Make a seasonal time line showing a penguin year. Divide the students into four groups and assign a season to each. Have each group remember what the King penguins do during their assigned time period. Give each group a large sheet of butcher paper. Have them label it with the season's name and months. (Remember the seasons are reversed in the Southern Hemisphere). Ask them to illustrate and write what the penguins are doing at that time of the year. When completed, join the four sections together and hang as a mural.

The chart below can be used as a guideline for the teacher.

Winter
(June, July, August)

Penguins swim, dive, and play in the sea. They eat many fish and get a layer of fat to keep them warm.

Spring
(Sept., Oct., Nov)

Penguins leave the ocean and waddle across the beach to find a mate. Females return to the sea to eat.

Summer
(Dec., Jan., Feb.)

Females return to the nest. Males go to sea for food. Sun shines day and night. Eggs hatch. Chicks join others at day nursery. Chicks grow a fine gray blanket of feathers.

Fall
(March, April, May)

Adult penguins return to the sea. They fatten up on fish, they wait for their feathers to molt. The young penguins splash into the water. They float far out to sea.

14

Making Comparisons

There are 17 species of penguins. Use pages 26-27 of the book *The Penguin* and the encyclopedia to find information about King penguins and Emperor penguins. Make a Venn diagram to compare them.

Emperor

Both

King

Drawing Conclusions

1. Little Penguin is sitting on the ice. Little Penguin wants something to eat. Little Penguin sees five fish in the sea. What will Little Penguin do?

_____

_____

_____

_____

2. Father Penguin is sitting on the nest. Mother Penguin has gone to the sea. Father Penguin wants to eat. He cannot leave Little Penguin. What will Father Penguin do?

_____

_____

_____

_____

3. Penguins play in the sea in the winter. Little Penguin has all of his feathers now. It will soon be winter at the South Pole. What will Little Penguin do?

_____

_____

_____

_____

Number the pictures to match the stories.

Readers' Theater

Readers' Theater is an exciting and relatively easy method of providing students with the opportunity to perform a mini-play without the hassle of props, sets, elaborate costumes, or memorization. Students read the dialogue of a character in a book or prepared script, or they can become the narrators to provide background information by reading the remaining words. The dialogue and narration may be read verbatim as the author has written it, or an elaboration may be written by the performing students. Sound effects and dramatic voices can make these much like radio plays.

A quick way to get started with this technique is to duplicate the desired pages directly from the book and have the students highlight their parts. Students should pare down the narration so that the emphasis is on dialogue. Meaning must be conveyed by voice, posture, and facial expression. Readers should be standing behind music stands or desks with the script in front of them. Often, the performers dress in black so even their dress does not distract from their verbal performance.

Little Penguin

Narrator:	Little Penguin was tired of living in his cold Antarctic home so one day he left to find a new home, First he went to Australia. He met a koala.
Little Penguin:	Mr. Koala, I'm looking for a new home. Would a penguin like to live In a koala's home?
Mr. Koala:	Can penguins climb trees?
Little Penguin:	I don't think so.
Mr. Koala:	Would penguins like to eat eucalyptus leaves?
Little Penguin:	Oh, no! Penguins like to eat fish.
Mr. Koala:	I don't think a penguin would like to live in a koala's home.
Narrator:	So Little Penguin went on until he met a kangaroo.
Little Penguin:	Mrs. Kangaroo, would a little penguin be happy in a kangaroo's home?
Mrs. Kangaroo:	Can penguins hop from place to place?
Little Penguin:	Oh no, Mrs. Kangaroo. Penguins waddle, slide, swim, and dive. They do not hop.
Mrs. Kangaroo:	Do penguins like to eat grass?
Little Penguin:	Oh no, Mrs. Kangaroo. Penguins only like to eat fish,
Mrs. Kangaroo:	I do not think you would fit in my pocket, Little Penguin. I do not think you would like a kangaroo home.
Narrator:	Little Penguin went back to the ocean. He swam to Africa. The first animal he met there was a monkey swinging from a tree.
Little Penguin:	Little Monkey, Little Monkey, would a penguin like to live in a monkey's home?

Readers' Theater *(cont)*

Monkey:	I do not think so Little Penguin. Can you swing from tree to tree and hang by your tall?
Little Penguin:	Oh no, Little Monkey. My tall is too small and my flippers are only good for swimming.
Monkey:	Do penguins like to eat bananas?
Little Penguin:	Oh no, Little Monkey. Penguins like to eat fish, lots of fish.
Monkey:	I do not think a penguin would like to live in my jungle home. Good-by, Little Penguin.
Narrator:	Little Penguin did not give up. He went along across Africa until he met an elephant. He looked up and shouted.
Little Penguin:	Mr. Elephant, would a little penguin be happy In an elephant's home?
Mr. Elephant:	Do penguins like to eat grass and trees?
Little Penguin:	Oh no, Mr. Elephant. Penguins like to eat lots of fish.
Mr. Elephant:	I do not think a little penguin would be happy in an elephant's home.
Narrator:	Little Penguin walked on. He was getting warm. He was getting hungry. He was getting tired. The next animal he met was his mother.
Little Penguin:	Mother! Mother! What are you doing here?
Mother Penguin:	I have been looking all over for you! Please come home, Little Penguin. Penguins must make their homes where the water is cold and there are lots of fish.
Little Penguin:	You are right Mother. I cannot climb trees. I cannot hop. I cannot hang by my tall. I cannot fit In a pocket. I do not like to eat eucalyptus leaves, grass, bananas, or trees. I think our home in the Antarctic is the best place for me.
Narrator:	Mother Penguin gave Little Penguin a big hug.
Mother Penguin:	And you will always have a mother's flippers to keep you warm when you are cold, Little Penguin!

Extensions

1. Have students add dialogue for other animals around the world.

2. Using the map on page 59, color the areas where penguins live. Refer to map on page 25 of Little Penguin.

3. Create simple costumes for the animals to wear in the play. Headband costumes are easily prepared by adding ears to an appropriately-colored strip of construction paper stapled to fit the child's head. Makeup can be used to add the animal's facial features.

Fingerplay

Ten Little Penguins

Ten little penguins

Sliding on the ice.

My, oh my, don't they look nice?

Then one fell down and landed with a frown.

Nine little penguins

(Repeat until one penguin remains.)

One little penguin

Sliding on the ice.

My, oh my, doesn't he look nice?

Then he fell down and landed with a frown.

No more penguins sliding on the ice!

Place ten puppets on fingers. Recite poem. As each penguin falls down, fold finger down or remove puppet. Make a sliding motion with hand when penguins are "sliding on the ice." Shake head "no" on last line.

Since it ia a very simple shape, the children may want to make penguin puppets for each of their fingers. Cut out. Color the beak. Wrap bottom tab around fingers and tape to right size.

A Take Home Game

| Start / Winner | Tell the other players a penguin story. | Hug the oldest person in the room and say, "I love you." |

Start

Winner

Do the penguin "waddle" twice around the table.

Tell which is bigger, an emperor or a King penguin.

RULES

❏ The person with the most letters in his first name goes first.

❏ Shuffle the cards. The first player draws a card. If it is even-numbered, move ½ that number of spaces. If it is odd0numbered, move that number of spaces. If it is a face card, stay where you are.

❏ If you land on a space occupied by another player, you may eat his playing piece. He starts over.

Would you like to live in the Antarctic? Tell two reasons why or why not.

If you can name four words that rhyme with "snow", you may eat your playing piece and get a new one.

Attach page 21 here

PARENTS: Please take some time to play this penguin game with your child. You will need a deck of playing cards with the 7's and 9's removed. Provide edible playing pieces, such as miniature marshmallows, goldfish crackers, popcorn, or jelly beans.

Make up three penguin names that begin with the letter "p".	Eat your own playing piece. Return to start. Get a new playing piece.	Read correctly all the penguin words in this box. Go back one space for each one missed. **flippers winter** **molting ocean**
	Move ahead two spaces.	
	Eat an extra playing piece without using your hands, the way a penguin would.	
Say 4 words that could describe a penguin.	Read correctly all words in this box. Go ahead one space for each correct word. **Antarctic feathers** **shrimp chicks**	Switch places with any player on the board.

Mr. Popper's Penguins

by Richard and Florence Atwater

Summary

Mr. Popper, a housepainter and a dreamer, receives a penguin from his friend, Admiral Drake, a scientist on expedition to the South Pole. Although Mr. Popper has read a great deal about penguins, he is in for many surprises when he tries to raise one in Stillwater. Captain Cook is joined by another penguin named Greta. Contrary to scientific expectation; Greta lays ten eggs and the Poppers soon have a houseful of penguins. Keeping them fed and happy is very costly, so the Poppers train the penguins and they begin performing in theaters from coast to coast.

Meet the Authors

Richard Atwater was born in Chicago, Illinois. He graduated from the University of Chicago and later taught Greek at that University. He met his wife, Florence, while he was teaching. Richard Atwater was also a columnist for the *Chicago Tribune* and *Chicago Evening Post* newspapers. The Atwaters had two daughters. One of their daughters was responsible for Mr. Atwater's book because she objected to all the historical facts included in children's books at that time. Mr. Atwater became ill before he could finish writing his book, so Mrs. Atwater completed it. The book was first published in 1938 and was an immediate best seller. It has been translated into Italian, Dutch, German, Spanish, Swedish, and Japanese.

Sample Plan

Day 1
- complete setting the stages activities (page 23)
- Prepare for Listing for Details (page27)
- Read aloud first 5 chapters of *Mr. Popper's Penguins*
- Choose activities from page 24
- Music: Have You Ever Seen? (page 65)
- Calender activity (page 8)
- Math: Graph It (page 53)

Day 2
- Calender activity (page 8)
- Read aloud 5 more chapters
- Choose activities from page 24-25
- Pick a Pair of Skates (page 45)
- Math: Penguin Review Strips (page 10)
- Read all About It! (page 28)
- Science: Using Thermometers (page 58)

Day 3
- Calender activity (page 8)
- Read aloud 5 more chapters
- Choose activities from pages 25-26
- Do and discuss Race to the Antarctic(page 60)

- Play Pole Race game or demonstrate and send home (pages 61-64)
- Find Percy (page 47)
- Poetry (page 37)

Day 4
- Finish Reading *Mr. Popper's Penguins*
- Choose activities from page 26
- Calender activity (page 8)
- Noun Categories (page 29)
- Performing Penguins' Math (page 30)
- Name That State (page 31)
- Writing: Cold Cereal Stories (page 38)

Day 5
- Readers' Theater (pages 32-34)
- Write questions for *Mr. Popper's Penguins* (Use page 9)
- Vocabulary Bingo (page 46)
- Calender activity (page 8)
- Being Big Book (pages 38-39)
- Make ice cream (page 71)

Day 6
- Culminating Activity: Have a Black and White Day (pages 72-73)

Overview of Activities

1. Introduce the book by having your principal or secretary deliver a box to your room with your name and address on it and an Antarctic return address. Like Mr. Popper's box, it should have air holes punched in it and "Air Express," "Keep Cool," and "Open at Once" written on the outside. Inside can be a stuffed penguin and the book, *Mr. Popper's Penguins.* The class can decide on a name for their new "pet" and can take turns taking it home overnight along with a journal to record the evening's events.

2. Locate Antarctica on a map and globe.

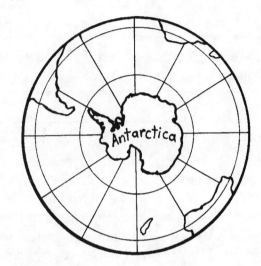

3. The authors tell us that Mr. Popper lived at 432 Proudfoot Avenue in Stillwater; but they do not tell us in what state or country. Have students use an atlas to find out where cities named Stillwater are located. Give each student an envelope. Have them address the envelope to themselves and put Mr. Popper's address where the return address belongs. These envelopes can be used for storing unit vocabulary cards, writing, or other materials.

ENJOYING THE BOOK

1. Begin reading *Mr. Popper's Penguins* to the class. There are 20 chapters in the book; so if four or five are read each day, the book can easily be completed in a school week.

2. Suggestions for discussion, writing topics, and/or activities for specific chapters will be found on pages 24-26.

EXTENDING THE BOOK

1. To review penguin facts follow the directions on page 38 to make a group Big Book, *All About Penguins.*

2. Have each child imagine having a penguin for a pet and write a story about it. Make penguins to hold these stories. Directions for the paper holders will be found on pages 66 and 67.

3. Complete page 60, Race to the Antarctic, together. Discuss. Duplicate and play the Pole Race game (see pages 61-62). Then send it home to be played with family for homework.

4. Make penguin ornaments from clay and paint them. See page 69 for this and other art suggestions.

5. To celebrate and culminate the penguin unit, have a Black and White Day. Plan a Penguin Performance. Make and send invitations. Share projects completed during the unit, perform Readers' Theater and unit songs, and enjoy simple refreshments with parents, another class, or school staff. (See page 72 for detailed suggestions.)

Using Mr. Popper's Penguins

Chapter I

1. Identify the characters and setting of the story.
2. What does Mr. Popper do for a living? What does he dream of doing?
3. Mr. Popper's work is seasonal. What does that mean? What other kinds of work are seasonal?
4. Compare the price of roast beef for four people to the price of beans for four people.

Chapter II

1. Locate the North and South Poles on a globe. Research the animals found near each.
2. What will Mr. Popper's surprise be? How will it be delivered? Draw a picture of your prediction.

Chapter III

1. Stop at appropriate places to have students refine their predictions about what will be in the box Mr. Popper receives and to suggest names for the penguin. They should tell why they choose a particular name.
2. What size is the penguin? What kind of penguin might it be?
3. Study where birds' eyes are located on their heads. Research how this affects the way birds see.
4. Discuss what the Poppers will have to do to care for a penguin.
5. Use the Listening for Details activity on page 27.

Chapter IV

1. Why is the penguin named Captain Cook? Research the real Captain Cook (James Cook, British navigator).
2. What do the Poppers try to feed Captain Cook? What does he eat? What do real penguins eat?

Chapter V

1. Read the first paragraph. Why is this such a good introduction to this chapter? (It makes you want to read the chapter.)
2. Mr. Popper pays the refrigerator service man $5.00. This book was written in 1938. Find out what a repairman charges today.
3. Why does the repairman think Mr. Popper is so strange?

Chapter VI

1. Why does the policeman come to the Poppers'?
2. What happens when Mr. Popper tries to get a license for the penguin? Use toy telephones to reenact the phone conversations.

Using Mr. Popper's Penguins *(cont.)*

Chapter VII

1. Discuss the role of women as portrayed in this 1938 book. Is it different today?
2. What does the penguin do while Mrs. Popper washes the dishes?
3. How does Mr. Popper dress when he goes for a walk with Captain Cook? Begin to plan for a Black and White Day (see page 72).

Chapter VIII

1. Make a map of the walk. Mark where people were met.
2. Write the newspaper article the reporter might have written. Draw the picture the photographer took. Make a class newspaper of the articles and pictures. Use page 28 as a starter.
3. Read the last sentence. What part of the sentence leads the reader to anticipate that something will happen in the barbershop? (". . . up to this time. . . ") What might happen?

Chapter IX

1. How does the man from the barber chair look when he runs into the street? What might he be saying? Make a cartoon drawing with speech bubble for this scene.
2. Where do Mr. Popper and the penguin go when they leave the barbershop? Why? What happens?

Chapter X

1. What do you think is wrong with Captain Cook?
2. How does Greta come to live with the Poppers?

Chapter XI

1. How do the Poppers tell the penguins apart? Think of some other ways that they could have done this.
2. Is the icy, snowy living room scene something that could really happen? Is it likely?

Chapter XII

1. The eggs are laid every third day. How many days until all ten are laid? Use a calendar to help.
2. How are the eggs incubated? How do penguins usually incubate their eggs?
3. List the names of all twelve penguins. Place them in alphabetical order.

Chapter XIII

1. The Poppers have money worries because the fish the penguins eat are very expensive. For homework have the children find out the price of at least one kind of fish. Have them compute how much it would cost each day to serve each of the ten penguins three pounds of fish. How much would it cost for a week, etc.?
2. Why do the Poppers decide to train the penguins?
3. Listen to Schubert's "Military March" and the "Merry Widow Waltz." Why is this music good for the activities the penguins do when they are played? Find other *marching, fighting,* and *tobogganing* music.

Using Mr. Popper's Penguins *(cont.)*

Chapter XIV

1. What do you think the passengers on the bus said when the penguins got on?
2. Practice combinations of 12 by setting up formations for the penguins. Figure how many eyes, flippers, and/or feet they have altogether.

Chapter XV

1. How do the penguins happen to be able to do their first performance?
2. How much money will Popper's Performing Penguins make in ten weeks?

Chapter XVI

1. Discuss the train vocabulary used in this chapter.
2. Use a United States map to begin tracing the route of the tour.

Chapter XVII

1. What products would penguins endorse? What famous people do you know that endorse products in commercials? Make up and perform commercials for the penguins.
2. What unexpected expenditures do the Poppers have on the trip? Use Performing Penguins' Math, page 30.
3. Complete the map of the trip and use page 31.

Chapter XVIII

1. Why don't the Poppers use air conditioning in the hotels where they stay? When and by whom was it invented?
2. What error does Mr. Popper make that causes so much trouble? What happens as a result of his error?
3. Make police and firemen hats. Use them to reenact the scene.

Chapter XIX

1. What is bail? How much is Mr. Popper's and the penguins' bail altogether? Who posts bail for them?
2. Locate the Arctic and Antarctica. Learn which is located at which Pole.
3. What will Mr. Popper decide? Write an ending for the story using your prediction.

Chapter XX

1. Why is Mr. Popper "pale and haggard"? What hard decisions have you had to make?
2. What is the purpose of the Expedition? Do you think it will succeed? Tell why or why not.
3. The sailors say, " 'It looks as if this will be a pretty lively trip'. . . " Write a sequel to the book telling what happens on the trip.
4. Work together to make a time line of the story. Record one event from each chapter of the story on the stomach of a penguin. (Use the pattern on page 74.) Join the flippers of all the penguins with paper fasteners and you will have 20 penguins on parade.

Listening for Details

Cut out the square on this page. Fold in all four corners on the dashed lines so the tips meet at the center point and the title and questions are on the outside. You will now have a smaller square. Write the title of the story you are reading on the title line. Put down your pencil when you are finished and be a very good listener or reader so you will be able to open each flap and answer the four questions on the *inside*.

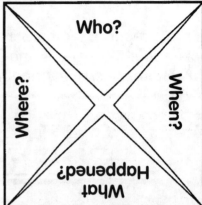

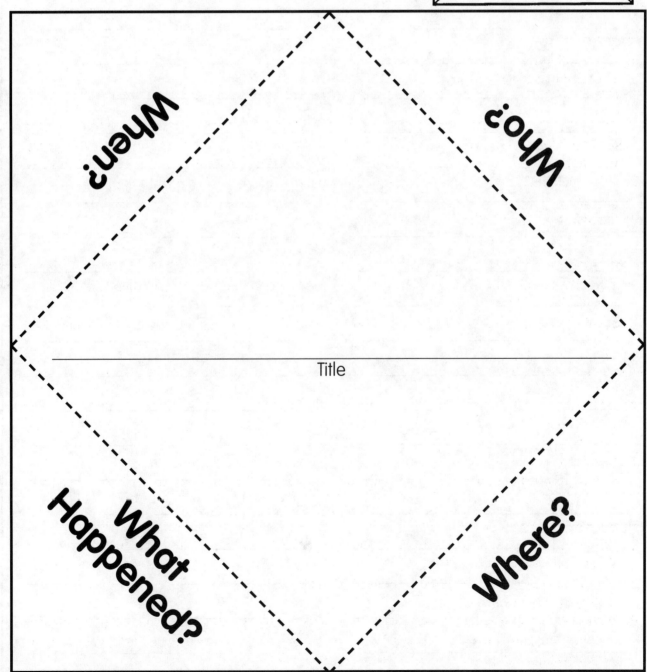

Title

Read All About It!

You are a reporter for the Stillwater Star News. You have been assigned to write a news article about Mr. Popper and his penguins. Be sure to include all the facts about who, what, where, when, why, and how. Write your story for the newspaper on the lines below.

Stillwater Star News

_____   _____

_____   _____

_____   _____

_____   _____

_____   _____

_____   _____

_____   _____

_____   _____

_____   _____

_____   _____

_____   _____

_____   _____

_____   _____

_____   _____

_____   _____

Name _____

Noun Categories

Using the book, *Mr. Popper's Penguins*, list at least six more nouns to fit into the following categories.

Person	Place	Thing
1. Mrs. Popper	1. Stillwater	1. ice
2. policeman	2. Milwaukee	2. hotels
3.	3.	3.
4.	4.	4.
5.	5.	5.
6.	6.	6.
7.	7.	7.
8.	8.	8.

Performing Penguins' Math

1. It cost Mr. Popper $950 to stay one week at the Tower Hotel in New York City. How much of his $1,500 will he have left after paying his hotel bill?

2. Mr. Popper had lunch at the hotel. it cost $2.50 for his hamburger, 75¢ for his milk and $1.75 for his dessert. How much did he spend for lunch?

3. Mrs, Popper needed new gloves before the next show. Mr. Popper gave her $20.00. She bought a pair for $8.76. How much money did she have left?

4. Mr. Popper ordered ice cream for the penguins twice. The first time it cost $47.56 and the second time $32.45. How much did Mr. Popper spend on ice cream that week?

Name _____

Name That State

Mr. Popper's Performing Penguins visited the states of Washington, New York, Minnesota, Pennsylvania, Wisconsin, Ohio, Illinois, and Michigan. The cities they visited are on the correct state shape. Can you name each state on the line below it? You may need to look on a big map of the United States.

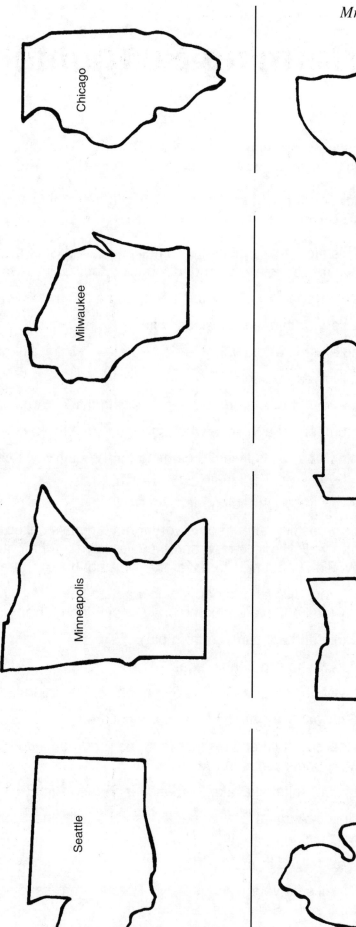

Readers' Theater

See page 17 for an introduction to Readers' Theater.

Many parts of *Mr. Popper's Penguins* are suitable for Readers' Theater. For example, chapters 6, 8, 14, and 15 contain much dialogue and many characters. Or, you may choose to use the script below.

Characters: Narrator, Mr. Popper, Mrs. Popper, Janie, Bill, Admiral Drake, Delivery Man, Veterinarian, Penguin Chorus

Narrator:	This story takes place in a small city called Stillwater. The characters are: (Characters step forward introducing themselves when called.)
Mr. Popper:	a housepainter, a penguin lover, and a dreamer
Mrs. Popper:	a very understanding housewife
Janie:	an eight year old daughter
Bill:	a ten year old son
Admiral Drake:	the leader of a group of men studying the Antarctic
Penguin Chorus:	members of audience who respond with "Gook, Gook" when indicated
Narrator:	Mr. Popper has finished painting for the day. He is sitting in his chair reading a book called *Antarctic Adventures.*
Mrs. Popper:	What are you reading, dear?
Mr. Popper:	I am reading about some very funny animals called penguins. They stand up and walk like little men and they lie down on their stomachs and slide. Wouldn't it be nice to have one for a pet?
Mrs. Popper:	Oh my! Bill wants a dog, Janie wants a kitten. And now you want a penguin! We do not have enough money to buy food for animals.
Narrator:	Janie and Bill come in from play.
Bill:	Are we having beans, again?
Janie:	I wish it was Sunday so we could have ice cream!
Mrs. Popper:	Go wash your hands for supper, children.
Narrator:	After the children finish their supper and homework, they go off to bed while Mr. Popper tunes in the radio.
Mr. Popper:	Listen, Admiral Drake is speaking on the radio.
Admiral Drake:	This is Admiral Drake speaking to you from the South Pole. Hello, Mr. Popper up there in Stillwater.
Mr. Popper:	He's talking to me!
Admiral Drake:	Thanks for your nice letter, Mr. Popper. I am sending you a surprise. Watch for it soon. Signing off. Signing off.

Readers' Theater *(cont.)*

Narrator: The next day a very large package is delivered to the Popper house. (Ring! Ring!)

Delivery Man: Does someone by the name of Popper live here?

Mr. Popper: That's me.

Delivery Man: Well, here is a package for you all the way from the Antarctic. Now that is some journey!

Janie: What is it, Papa?

Bill: It says, "Unpack at once" and "Keep cool" on the outside.

Narrator: When Mr. Popper opens the crate, out steps a little penguin about two and a half feet tall.

Penguin Chorus: Gook! Gook!

Janie and Bill: Papa, what is it?

Mr. Popper: It is a penguin sent to me from the South Pole by Admiral Drake.

Narrator: The penguin is very curious. He marches all over the house.

Penguin Chorus: Gook! Gook!

Janie: Can we keep him, Papa?

Bill: What shall we name him?

Narrator: Mrs. Popper has just returned home from a meeting. She hasn't seen the penguin yet.

Mr. Popper: Let's call him Captain Cook.

Mrs. Popper: Call who Captain Cook?

Narrator: With a flap of his flippers Captain Cook jumps down to the floor, walks over to Mrs. Popper, and begins to peck at her ankle.

Mrs. Popper: Help! Help!

Narrator: Mrs, Popper runs Into the kitchen and so does the penguin. When he sees the refrigerator, he stops and tries to open it.

Penguin Chorus: Gook! Gook!

Narrator: Mrs. Popper offers him some food but he doesn't seem to be hungry. A few minutes later —

Bill: Mamal Papal Come see what Captain Cook has done!

Narrator: Captain Cook has found the goldfish bowl and helped himself to supper.

Readers' Theater *(cont.)*

Janie:	Bad, bad penguin!
Penguin Chorus:	Gook! Gook!
Narrator:	Captain Cook waddles quickly out to the kitchen and climbs into the open refrigerator.
Mr. Popper:	He needs a cold place. We can let him sleep in the refrigerator at night with the door open.
Narrator:	Soon the whole town knows about Captain Cook. The newspaper reporters all come to take pictures.
Janie:	Papa, Captain Cook does not look happy.
Bill:	I think he is sick, Papa. Let's ask the veterinarian to help.
Veterinarian:	I will give you some pills for him. Feed him ice cream and wrap him in ice packs. Our weather is not cold enough for him. He may not get well.
Narrator:	A man at a big aquarium hears about the sick Captain Cook. He also has a sick penguin named Greta.
Veterinarian:	Maybe the two penguins are just lonely. Let's ask if Greta can come to visit Captain Cook.
Narrator:	Greta comes to live with the Poppers and now there are two happy penguins in the refrigerator.
Mr. Popper:	Now that winter is here we can open all the windows and it will be cold enough in the house for the penguins.
Narrator:	The Popper family has to wear their coats, hats, and mittens in the house to keep *warm*.
Janie:	Papa! Papa! Come quick! Greta laid an egg.
Narrator:	Three days later.
Bill:	Papa! Papa! Look, Greta has laid another egg.
Narrator:	Mr. Popper later finds Greta has ten eggs in her nest!
Mr. Popper:	I can't understand this! Everyone knows penguins never lay more than two eggs a year.
Mrs. Popper:	Well, someone must have forgotten to tell Greta. Whatever will we do with ten penguin chicks?
Penguin Chorus:	Gook! Gook! Gook! Gook! Gook! Gook! Gook! Gook! Gook! Gook!
Narrator:	Soon, Mr. Popper and his penguins are asked to appear in a show. They call it *Popper's Performing Penguins.* The penguins love the bright lights and crowds and the Poppers will never have to worry about money.
Janie and Bill:	Now we can have ice cream every day of the week!

Name _____   *Poetry & Writing*

Penguin Poems

Read the penguin poetry below. Write the missing words. Try writing some rhymes of your own.

I like penguins

I like their looks

I like to read

About them in _____.

Penguins eat fish

And swim a lot,

The penguin's home

Is never _____.

I like penguins wet,

I like penguins dry,

I'd like to watch one

Try to _____.

In the sea's where

Penguins like to play,

So please, Mr. Hunter,

Stay _____.

Penguins are cute

And lots of fun.

They can walk

But they can't_____.

Penguins swim in the ocean.

Penguins swim in the sea.

Penguins swim faster

Than you or _____.

Extension: Cut these out. Glue to larger paper and illustrate.

Penguin Poems *(cont.)*

Read the penguin poetry below. Write the missing words. Try writing some rhymes of your own.

Penguins play in the ocean

Penguins fish in the _____.

Penguins lay their eggs

In a *stony*_____.

Penguins find a mate

And build a _____.

They work hard

And then they _____.

Penguins play in the ocean

Penguins slide on the _____.

I think penguins

Are very _____.

Penguins like the ice.

Penguins like the_____.

Penguins don't mind

When the cold winds _____

When a penguin's hungry,

He eats _____.

He doesn't need a fork.

And he doesn't need a_____

Penguins are black.

Penguins are_____.

Penguins are the colors

Of day and _____.

Extension: Record these rhymes and the ones that the children create on chart paper. Chant them together for oral reading fun.

Writing Penguin Poetry

Diamante

A diamante poem has seven lines and does not rhyme. It is shaped like a diamond. Use the directions and model below to create a penguin diamante.

Line 1 –

one word – noun

Line 2 –

two words – adjectives

Line 3 –

three words – "ing" verbs

Line 4 –

four words – nouns

Line 5 –

three words – "ing" verb

Line 6 –

two words – adjectives

Line 7 –

one word – a synonym for the first noun

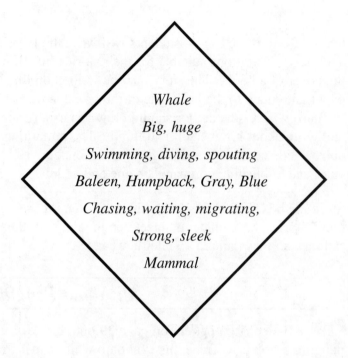

Whale
Big, huge
Swimming, diving, spouting
Baleen, Humpback, Gray, Blue
Chasing, waiting, migrating,
Strong, sleek
Mammal

Acrostic

Write a penguin poetry acrostic by printing "penguins" down the side of a piece of paper, one letter per line. Start each line of the poem with these letters. Try single words or phrases. A dictionary would be very useful. Here are two examples:

Perky
Exciting
Nodding
Growing
Unbelievable
Interesting
Nest-building
Swimmers.

Parading penguins,
Each one soon
Nesting on the cold
Ground with stones
Underneath and
In between for a
Nest. It is
Spring in Antarctica.

Penguin Writing Activities

Cold Cereal Stories

Ask parents to help their child cover all four sides of an empty cereal box with brown paper (insides of paper grocery sacks work just fine). Have students bring them to school to use for writing "cool penguin stories."

On the front of the boxes, students will write the titles and draw illustrations suitable for their stories (much like the cover of a book). The story may be written on lined paper and glued to the back side of the box. On one of the narrow sides the author should draw a self-portrait and write about him/herself and family. The remaining narrow side could be used for the dedication, copyright year, and publishing company's name and address.

Store the boxes on a classroom shelf. To share these cool" stories, have students select one to take with them to lunch so they can read while they eat.

All About Penguins Big Book

Enlarge the penguin pattern on page 39 onto black poster board. Cut a large oval pattern to fit the penguin's stomach. Trace this oval onto white paper for book pages. Use one oval as the title page — "All About Penguins."

Divide the class into several small groups. Assign each group a topic such as habitat, enemies, food, physical characteristics, babies, or habits. Each group should research, plan, and write their information and an illustration on one of the white ovals.

Prepare an author page with duplicated photographs of the children (or self-portraits) and their signatures. They may even want a dedication page. With the title page on top, attach the "stomachs" to the penguin with large paper fasteners.

Share your Big Book with another class when it is completed or ask the librarian to display it on a library table with other penguin books.

Big Book Pattern

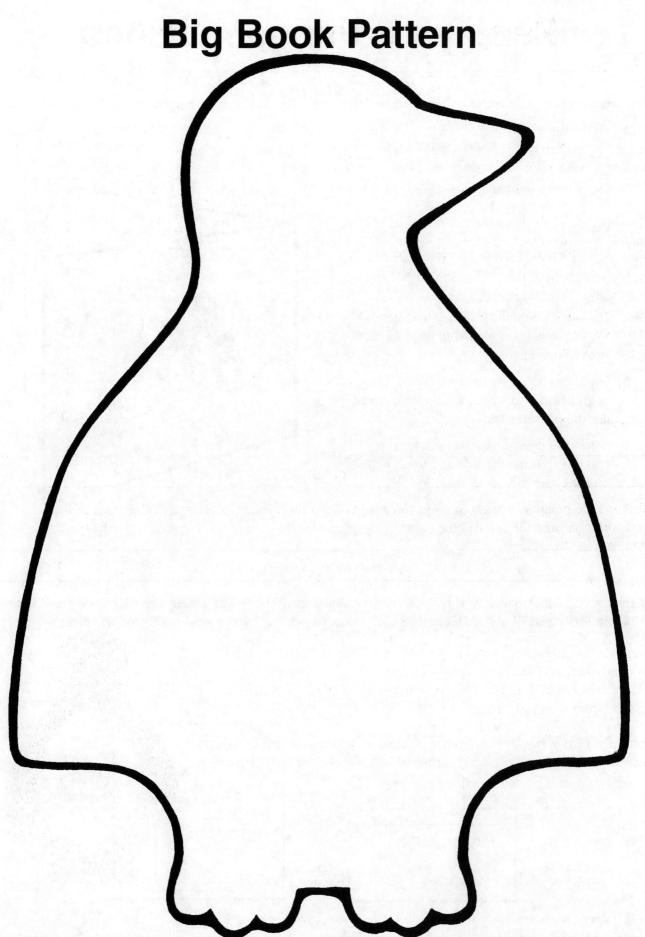

Displaying Penguin Writing

A Snow Scene Book Cover

1. Fold a 12" X 18" (30 cm X 45 cm) sheet of dark blue construction paper in half to form a book cover.

2. Cut a wavy pattern across a 9" X 12" (22.5 cm X 30 cm) sheet of white paper to suggest a snowdrift.

3. Glue the white paper over the blue with the bottom edges even to make a snow-covered hillside.

4. Cut out a penguin (you may use the finger puppet penguin from page 19) and glue it in the snow.

5. Dip the pointed wooden handle of a paint brush into white liquid tempera and dot the picture with "snow."

6. When the paint is dry, use markers or crayons to write the title and your name on the cover you have made.

7. Write a penguin poem or short story to place inside the folded blue paper.

A Writing Hang Up

Cover wire clothes hangers with black construction paper to simulate tuxedos as pictured below. Have students write and illustrate short stories or poems on white paper to be mounted on the black "tuxedos."

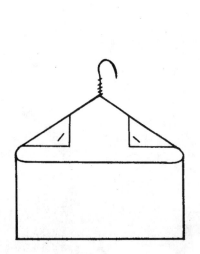

Additional Literature Suggestions

1. Read *The Important Book* by Margaret Wise Brown.

   Using the book's language pattern, students will write "The Important Thing About Penguins." For example:

   The important thing about penguins is they live in the Antarctic. They are black and white. They eat fish. They can swim very fast. Their babies are called chicks. But the important thing about penguins is they live in the Antarctic.

2. Read *A Snowy Day* by Ezra Jack Keats.

   Have students follow these directions to create "A Snowy Day" picture: Cut out a large penguin and glue it to a dark blue piece of construction paper. Dip a toothbrush into thick white tempera paint, blot on a paper towel, and then draw it across a small piece of window screen held over the penguin paper to spatter white all over your picture. Now write some sentences or a story about your snow-covered penguin.

3. Read *A Cache of Jewels* by Ruth Heller.

   In this beautifully-illustrated book the children will learn that a group of penguins is a parcel, many peacocks make a muster, and many whales a gam. Have them name and illustrate other collective nouns.

4. Read *Antarctica* by Helen Cowcher.

   To help protect Antarctica for the penguins, write to:
     The Cousteau Society
     930 West 21st Street
     Norfolk, Virginia 23517

   Share feelings or create a drawing or slogan about Antarctica. Send these to:
     Antarctic Mailbag
     National Geographic World
     Washington, D.C. 20036

5. Read *"What Is Black?"* and *"What Is White?"* from *Hailstones and Halibut Bones* by Mary O'Neill.

   After reading the poems, write "White is…" on a large sheet of white paper and "Black is…" on a large sheet of black paper (use chalk). Record or have the children record their suggestions for completing the sentences.

6. Read several selections from Eric Carle's *Animals, Animals* including the penguin poem, **"Enigma Sartorial."**

   Observe and duplicate the tissue paper and paint technique used for the illustrations.

   Select from the following activities to use with some or all of the 74 animals represented in this book. Categorize them into land or sea animals or fish, reptiles, mammals, or birds. List the endangered animals. List the farm or jungle animals. When lists are complete, alphabetize them. Have groups of children illustrate the lists and display.

Additional Literature Suggestions

7. Read *Tacky the Penguin* by Helen Lester.

   Have a fun discussion about how Tacky's being different from the crowd helped his fellow penguins.

   Note the chant repeated by the hunters in the story. Have children create their own poetic chants. Here is an example:

   Penguin, penguin, what shall we do?
   Swim in the ocean where the water's blue!

   Penguin, penguin, where shall we go?
   Back to the rookery, all in a row!

   Penguin, penguin, what will we see?
   Ice and snow and penguins like me!

   Penguin, penguin, I don't like fish!
   Then you may eat whatever you wish!

   Record the chant on chart paper. Divide the class into two groups. Take turns reading alternate lines.

   Give the children small paper squares. (Sticky notes work well.) Have them draw their favorite foods and sign their names. Prepare a chart with various categories of food and have children attach their papers in the appropriate column for a Favorite Foods Graph.

8. Read *Little Penguin's Tale* by Audrey Wood.

   This book shows how stories can have more than one ending. Ask students to suggest alternative endings to some of the penguin stories you have shared.

   This book is also an excellent medium for introducing homonyms. Little Penguin does not want to listen to his Grand Nanny's "tales" and ends up almost losing his "tail." Divide the class into two teams and have them try to "catch" as many homonyms as possible in a specified number of days. Prepare a bulletin board as pictured below. Let each team name their penguin and write their homonyms on fish to attach to real string lines.

Name _____

Rhyming Penguins

If the words on the penguin's flippers rhyme, color the penguin. List all the words that do not rhyme on the back of this paper. Write a rhyming word for each word on your list.

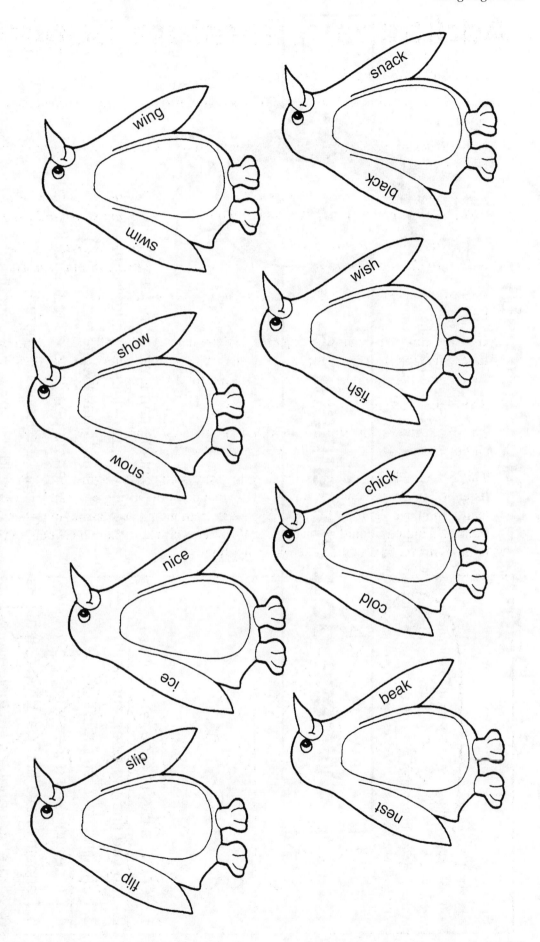

Punctuation Penguins

Make several sentence strips like the one pictured below out of oaktag or heavy paper. Laminate. Write asking or telling sentences on the laminated strips with a permanent marking pen. (It can be erased with nail polish remover or hair spray when you want to change the sentences.) Have the children put the correct punctuation mark on the penguin's tummy with an overhead projector pen. (It erases easily with water.) Use sentences below or others appropriate for your grade level.

Where do penguins live

1. Penguins like to slide on the ice(.)
2. Can you find the little penguin(?)
3. Penguins have strong beaks(.)
4. Do penguins use their wings to fly(?)
5. Penguins have black and white feathers(.)
6. Where do penguins lay their eggs(?)
7. Penguins feed fish to their chicks(.)
8. Watch out, here comes a skua gull(!)

9. Penguins can swim very fast(.)
10. How many kinds of penguins are there(?)
11. Penguins have white eye rings(.)
12. When do penguins go to the rookery(?)
13. Help, the ice is thin here(!)
14. Would you like a pet penguin(?)
15. What do penguins like to eat(?)
16. Whee, sliding on the ice is fun(!)

Place strips in a large manila envelope labeled "Punctuation Penguins." Place a separate answer sheet inside the envelope. Students must match the sentences to check their work.

Pick a Pair of Skates

Choose eight crayons. Color the skates with related words the same color.

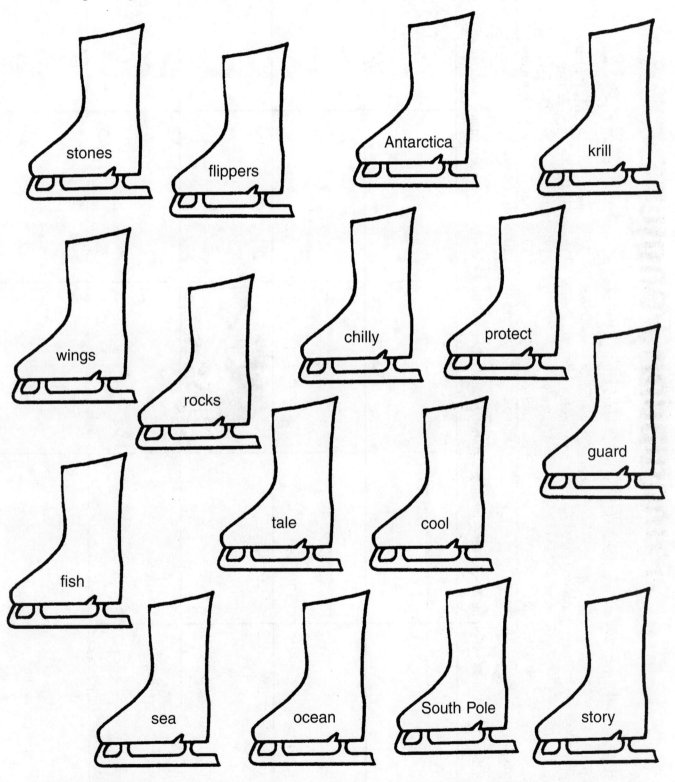

Choose one word from each pair to use in an asking sentence. Write your sentence on the back of this paper

Vocabulary Bingo

Have students place the following vocabulary words in random order on the bingo grid.

1. South Pole
2. flippers
3. tuxedos
4. stones
5. blizzards

6. Antarctic
7. ocean
8. waddle
9. chick
10. snow

11. penguins
12. diving
13. colony
14. hatch
15. molt

16. emperor
17. swimming
18. skua
19. winter
20. temperature

21. feathers
22. slide
23. nests
24. weather

Winner calls out "Ark-ark" when he or she gets five in a row horizontally, diagonally, or vertically Penguin space is a free space.

Find Percy

Follow the directions to find Percy, the penguin, on this page.

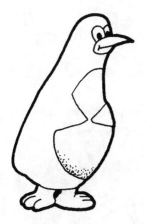

1. Percy is large.

2. Percy is wearing a scarf.

3. Percy has only one flipper showing.

4. Percy has three toes on each foot.

5. Percy does not have on a hat.

6. Percy is 2½ inches tall.

7. Percy is near the right edge of this paper.

8. Percy does not have a bow tie,

9. Percy's eyes are closed.

10. Color Percy black, white, and orange and his scarf red.

On the back of this paper draw two penguins talking to each other. In bubbles ⟨ ⟩ above their heads write what they are saying to each other.

More Language Activities

Posting Vowels to Penguins

Cut ten or more stamp-sized pieces of paper with pinking shears. Write a, e, i, o, or u on each stamp and indicate whether it should be long or short. Have each child select a stamp and glue it in the proper place on an envelope. Using old magazines, newspapers, junk mail, etc., the children should select pictures with their vowel sound and place those pictures inside the envelope.

Envelopes can then be addressed to a penguin friend.

The following addresses can be used or the children can create their own.

Paul Penguin
1234 Frozen Avenue
Freezer City, Minnesota 50437

Paula Penguin
325 Snowflake Drive
Antarctic City, Maine 63259

Patty Penguin
525 Flipper Lane
Coldtown, Iowa 50070

Have students deliver their "mail" to other students for reading and checking.

Alliteration

Have children write and illustrate sentences beginning with as many "p" words as possible.

Examples   *Pretty penguins paraded past the post office.*
                Perky penguins wore pajamas to the party.
                Playful penguins played the piano.

Penguin Vocabulary Card Game

Make a deck of word cards approximately 3" x 5" (7.5 cm x 12.5 cm). On the front side of each card write one vocabulary word. On the back side put a penguin sticker and one letter of the word "penguin." Make enough cards so that it is possible to spell penguin several times.

Place the deck of cards in the center of a table with the vocabulary word facing up. Students take turns drawing the top card. If they can pronounce the word and use it in a sentence, they may keep the card. Students check letters on the back of the "keep" card and try to be the first one to spell the word "penguin." When one student has all seven cards needed, he/she shouts, "Penguin Parade," and wins the game. The rest of the students must waddle around the table!

Penguin Number Book

sample page

Reproduce this pattern an appropriate number of times. Write, or have students write, a number word and its matching numeral on the feet and/or on the flippers of the penguin. Illustrate or write about the number on the stomach. Assemble completed pages into a number booklet.

Snack Attack

Help Pete Penguin catch some lunch. Solve the problems on the fish. On the back, draw and label your favorite snack!

Note to Teacher: Program fish with number facts appropriate to grade level.

Penguin Open Worksheet

Color all penguins with even-numbered answers.

Give all the colored penguins names beginning with "p."

Teacher: Program the penguins to coincide with the math skill currently being taught.

Money Matters

Counting Change

Cut this penguin out of black and white construction paper. Give him an orange beak and orange feet. On his white stomach stamp or glue paper coins in a variety of amounts. Write the correct amounts on the fish shapes. Laminate and place several in a center. Children must count the coins and match with the fish of the same amount. Make these self-correcting by putting the correct amount in white ink on the back of the penguin or number and provide an answer sheet.

Shopping for Fish

Have students collect and bring clean, empty tuna fish cans. Let them design labels for the cans with the price clearly marked on them. Play store. Give each student some play money to "shop" for food for their pet penguin. Let them count back the correct change.

Graph It

Provide goldfish-shaped crackers in at least 5 different flavors. Give students one cracker of each flavor. Ask them to taste each one and record their favorite on a scrap of paper. Have them place their papers in labeled piles on a table. Count the selections in each pile and make a bar graph showing "Favorite Fish."

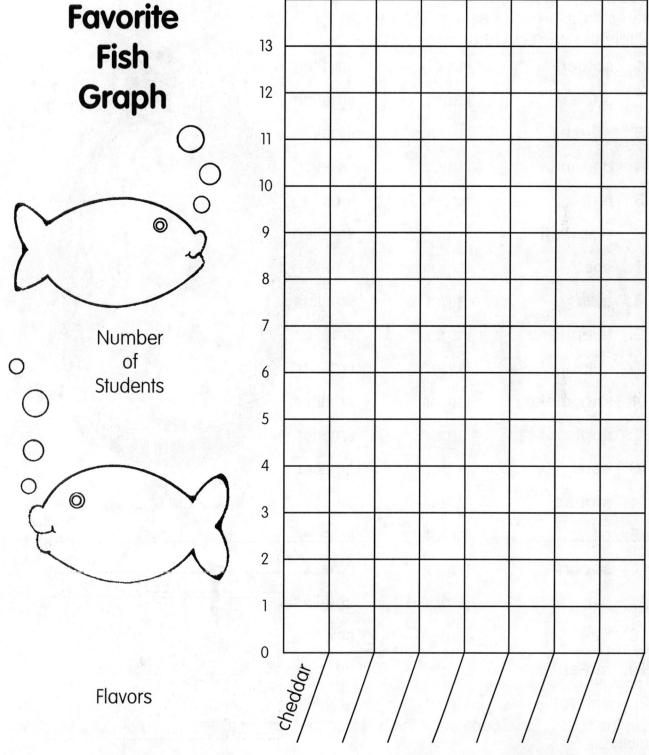

Favorite Fish Graph

Number of Students

Flavors

cheddar

Penguin Comparisons

An emperor penguin is the largest penguin. When full-grown, it stands about 4 feet (1.3 meters) high and weighs close to 100 pounds (45 kilograms). The Adéllie penguin is the most common penguin. It is only about 2 feet (60 cm) high and weighs about 11 pounds (5 kilograms).

Does the first word in each line describe something larger or smaller than a penguin? Circle the correct word.

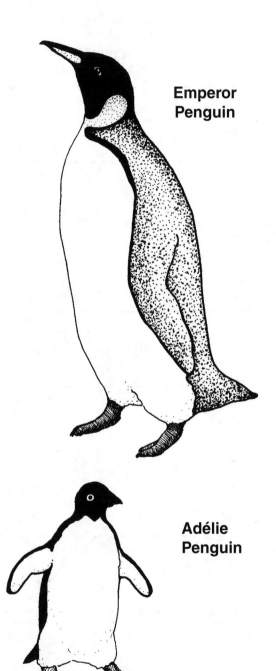

Emperor Penguin

Adélie Penguin

1.	**spider**	larger	smaller
2.	**shoe**	larger	smaller
3.	**house**	larger	smaller
4.	**banana**	larger	smaller
5.	**hat**	larger	smaller
6.	**elephant**	larger	smaller
7.	**seed**	larger	smaller
8.	**man**	larger	smaller
9.	**telephone**	larger	smaller
10.	**camel**	larger	smaller
11.	**snowflake**	larger	smaller
12.	**apple**	larger	smaller
13.	**barn**	larger	smaller
14.	**mouse**	larger	smaller
15.	**penny**	larger	smaller
16.	**spoon**	larger	smaller
17.	**car**	larger	smaller
18.	**bus**	larger	smaller
19.	**mitten**	larger	smaller
20.	**school**	larger	smaller

On the back of this page draw three things that are smaller than a penguin. Label your pictures.

ABC Birds

Put these nine birds in correct ABC order on the lines. Then choose one bird from the list to illustrate on the back of this paper. Use an encyclopedia to find some facts about the bird you have drawn. Write three factual sentences about your bird.

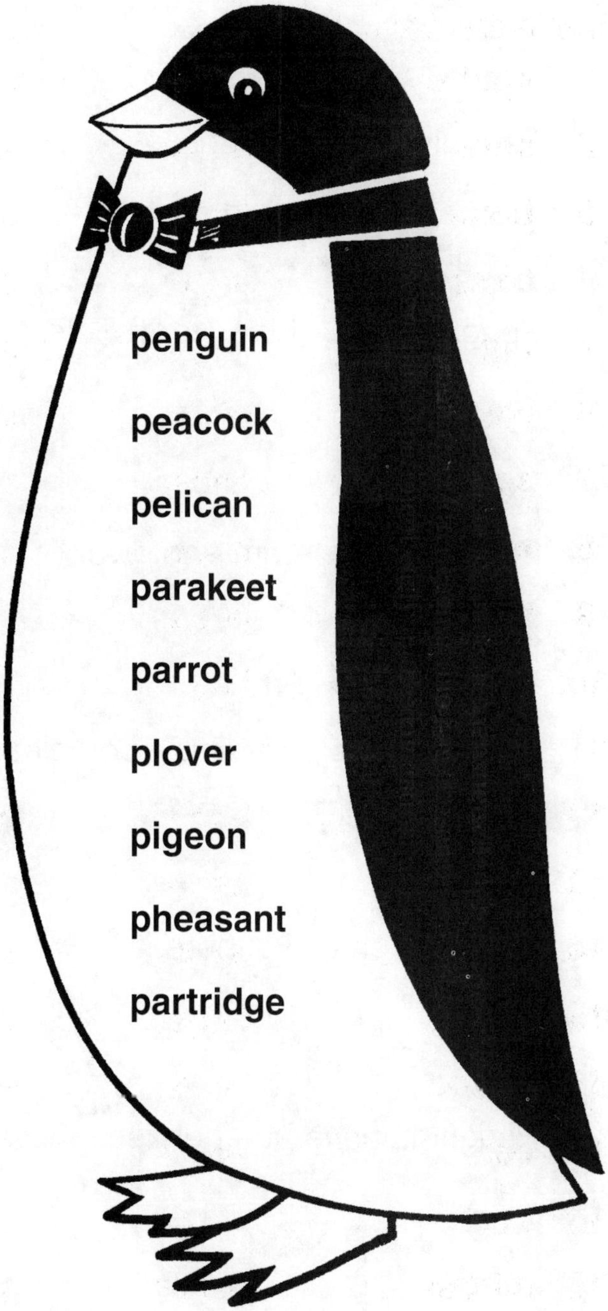

_____

_____

_____

_____

_____

_____

_____

_____

_____

penguin

peacock

pelican

parakeet

parrot

plover

pigeon

pheasant

partridge

True or False?

Cut out the faces on this page. If the sentence below could really happen or is true about penguins, glue a smiling face behind it. If it is not true and could not happen, glue a sad face behind it.

1. Penguins can fly.

2. Penguins can lay eggs.

3. Penguins live at the North Pole.

4. Penguins can swim and dive.

5. Penguins live together in colonies.

6. Penguins have feathers.

7. Penguins have no enemies.

8. Baby penguins are called chicks.

Thermometers

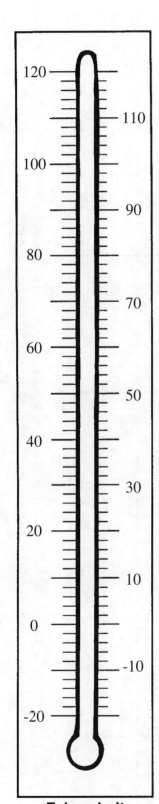

Thermometers tell us how cold it is.

Thermometers tell us how hot it is.

This is called the **temperature.**

Temperature is measured in **degrees.**

We use two kinds of **thermometers.**

Fahrenheit thermometers are like the one on the left side of this page. **Celsius thermometers** are like the one on the right side of the page.

Water freezes at 32 **degrees** on the **Fahrenheit thermometer,** Water freezes at **0 degrees** on the **Celsius thermometer.**

Some **thermometers** have **mercury** inside them. It is gray. Some **thermometers** have **alcohol** inside them. It is colored red.

With your *red* crayon make the alcohol in the **Fahrenheit thermometer** show the **temperature** of freezing.

With your *gray* crayon make the mercury in the **Celsius thermometer** show the **temperature** of freezing.

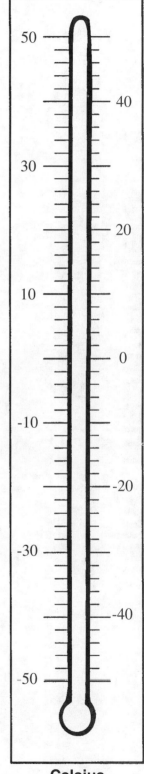

**Fahrenheit
Thermometer**

**Celsius
Thermometer**

Using Thermometers

Experiment 1: Divide the classroom into 4 or 5 groups. Number each group. Give each group a thermometer and an ice cube in a plastic self-closing bag. Have each group select a spot somewhere in the room to place their ice cube and their thermometer. After each group has chosen their location, ask for predictions as to which cube will be melted first. Record the predictions. Begin this experiment early in the day and check the cubes every fifteen minutes.

Scientific Log

Group Number	Prediction	Order of Melting	Temperature of Melting	Minutes

Experiment 2: Fill a glass with cold water . Predict its temperature. Measure and record its temperature with a thermometer. Fill a glass with hot water(from a faucet). Predict the temperature. Use a thermometer to measure and record its temperature.

Name _____

Where Do Penguins Live?

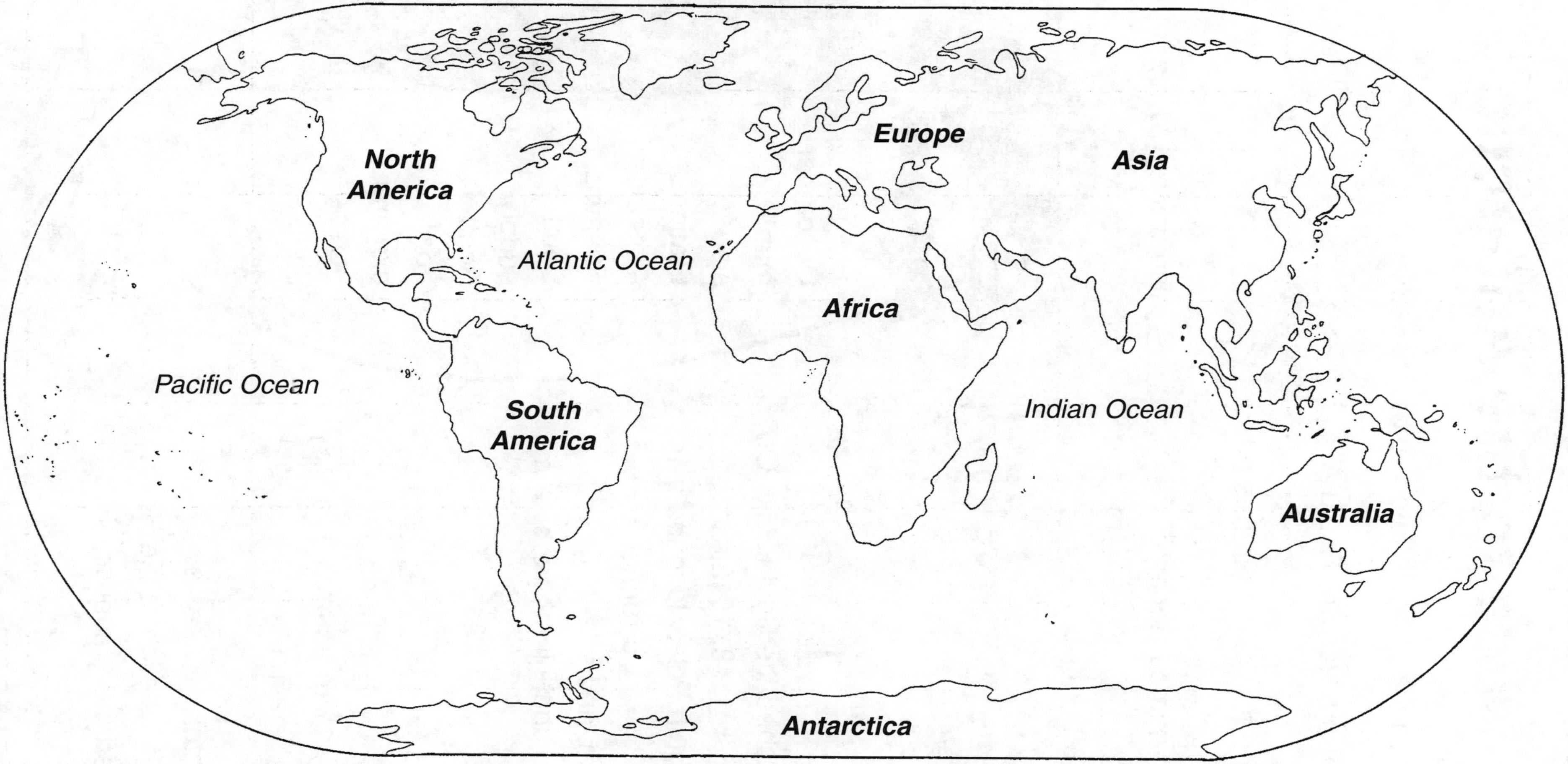

Asia

Europe

Australia

Indian Ocean

Africa

Atlantic Ocean

South America

North America

Antarctica

Pacific Ocean

How many oceans do you see? _____ Write their names on the back of this paper.

How many continents do you see? _____ Write their names on the back of this paper.

Color the continent where you live green.

Color where penguins live yellow.

Name_____
Science

Race to the Antarctic

Use the words on the penguin to complete this story.

In 1911 a man from Norway, Roald A __ u __ __ __ __ __ .

wanted to be the first person to reach the __ __ __ __ h Pole.

An Englishman named Robert F, S __ __ __ __ also wanted to be
the first __ x __ __ __ __ __ __ to
reach the South Pole.

Amundsen used __ o __ __ to pull his
sleds. Scott used
__ __ __ __ __ s.

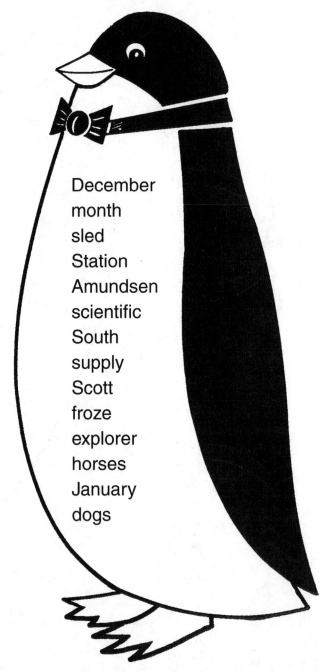

On __ __ __ e __ __ __ r 14,1911,
Amundsen reached the South Pole. On
__ __ __ u __ __ __ 18, 1912, Scott
reached the South Pole. He found a
flag tied to a __ __ __ d runner, a note
from Amundsen, and a tent,\.
Amundsen had beat him there by a m
__ __ __ __!

Scott and his crew __ r __ __ __ to
death on their way back home.
They were only 11 miles from a
s __ p __ __ __ station.

The United States now has a
s __ i __ n __ ific station at the South
Pole,. It is called the Amundsen-Scott

__ __ __ __ __ __ __ __ .

December
month
sled
Station
Amundsen
scientific
South
supply
Scott
froze
explorer
horses
January
dogs

#277 Thematic Unit—Penguins   60   © *Teacher Created Materials, Inc.*

Pole Race

Preparation: Reproduce the game board (pages 61-62), attach pieces, color, glue into a folder, and laminate (if desired). Duplicate the sentence cards on pages 63 - 64 onto heavy paper, laminate (if desired), and cut apart. **Rules:** Play in pairs or two teams. Put team markers at Start. Decide which way each team will go. The person with the birthday closest to January 1 begins by drawing and reading one of the sentence cards. When the card has been read correctly, count the number of words beginning with vowels on the card. Move that number of spaces. Teams and team members take turns drawing and reading cards. The first person or team to reach the South Pole by the exact number wins!

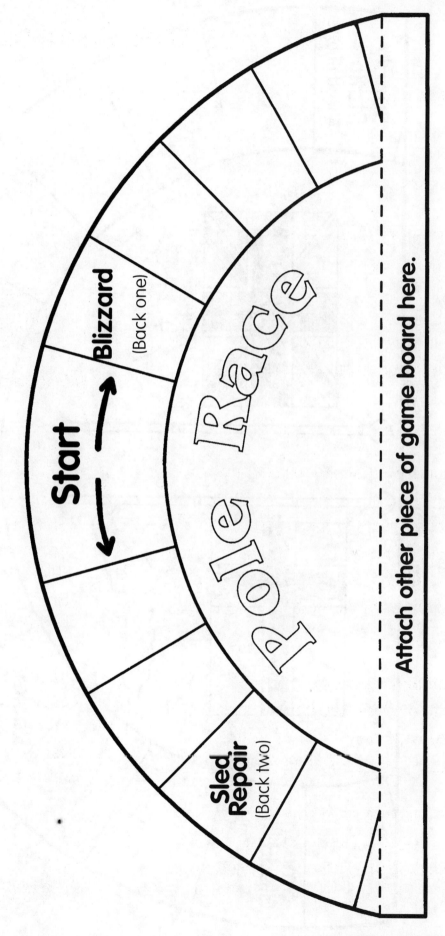

Start

Blizzard
(Back one)

Pole Race

Sled Repair
(Back two)

Attach other piece of game board here.

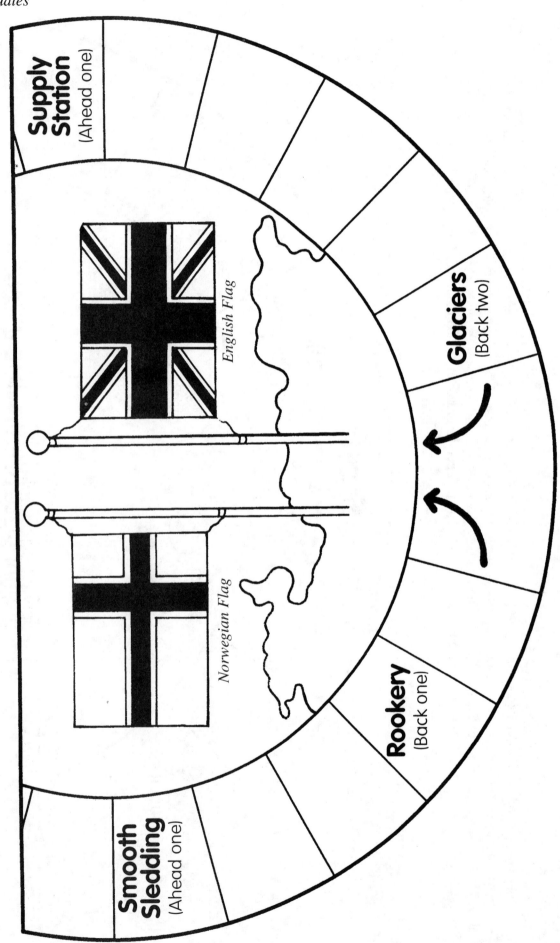

Supply Station (Ahead one)

English Flag

Norwegian Flag

Glaciers (Back two)

Rookery (Back one)

Smooth Sledding (Ahead one)

62

Game Cards

There is a scientific research station named Amundsen-Scott at the South Pole.	A day is six months long at the South Pole.	Antarctica covers 5,100,000 square miles.	Winter comes in July in Antarctica.
Antarctic animals depend on the sea for food.	Antarctica was once covered with trees and plants.	Robert F. Scott reached Antarctica 35 days after Amundsen.	An American named Richard Byrd led five groups to the Antarctic.
Horses pulled Robert F. Scott's sleds at the South Pole.	Amundsen's team reached the South Pole first.	Robert F. Scott used horses to pull his sled during the race.	Antarctica has many rivers of ice called glaciers.

Game Cards *(cont)*

Scientists study Antarctic ice caps to predict weather.	Penguins are among the many birds that live in Antarctica.	Amundsen used dogs to pull his sleds.	Antarctica is the fifth largest continent.
Now 3000 tourists visit Antarctica each year.	Tourists come to Antarctica to see the wildlife and scenery.	Richard Byrd was the first to fly an airplane over the South Pole.	Robert F. Scott was an Englishman.
Amundsen was from the country of Norway.	Antarctica is bigger than the United States.	The ice is sometimes two miles thick at the South Pole.	Antarctica sometimes has temperatures of 100° below zero.

64

Penguin Songs

"Have You Ever Seen a Penguin?"

(Tune: "Have You Ever Seen a Lassie?")

Have you ever seen a penguin, a penguin, a penguin?

Have you ever seen a penguin swim this way and that?

Swim this way and that way and this way and that way?

Have you ever seen a penguin swim this way and that?
(Make swimming motions with arms.)

Repeat, substituting " slide" for " swim."
(Make sliding motions with hands and feet.)

Repeat substituting "waddle" for "swim."
(Take tiny little steps, swinging bodies right and left.)

Repeat, substituting "dress" for "swim."
(Boys bow and girls curtsy.)

"Ten Little Penguins"

(Tune: "Ten Little Indians")

Have children form a large circle. Number the children to ten as many times as needed so that everyone has a number. Have the children sing the song below. As his/her number is sung the child with the matching number "waddles five steps like a penguin" toward the middle of the circle and turns to face the outside of the circle. When their number is sung during the second verse, all "penguins" walk back to their original place in the circle.

One little, two little, three little penguins,
Four little, five little, six little penguins,
Seven little, eight little, nine little penguins,
Ten little penguin chicks.

Ten little, nine little, eight little penguins,
Seven little, six little, five little penguins,
Four little, three little, two little penguins,
One little penguin chick.

Penguin Waddle Relay

Divide the class into two teams. Place half of each team behind lines 6 to 8 yards (6 to 7 meters) apart. Place a 6 to 8 inch (15 to 20 cm) rubber ball between the knees of the first two people in line and watch them waddle like penguins to give the ball to their teammates behind the opposite line. The teammates then carry the balls back to the starting line and the waddling continues until everyone has had a turn. If the ball is dropped, the penguin must go back to his/her starting point and begin again. The winning penguins are the ones that can waddle the fastest without losing the ball.

Variation: Do not use balls. Have students waddle to tag partner with arms at sides, hands tilted up, knees touching, and toes pointed slightly out.

Penguin Paper Holder

Cut out patterns on pages 66 and 67.

Fold a sheet of black construction paper in half the long way. Lay the body pattern on the black paper with the dotted line on the fold. Trace and cut out.

Cut beak from orange paper. Glue top edge of beak to penguin's head about 2½ inches (6.25 cm) down. Leave tip of beak unglued to form the holder for the top of an inserted paper.

Cut feet from orange paper. Open penguin and glue feet at heels to penguin body. Leave the toes unglued to hold bottom of inserted papers.

Cut black and white circles for eyes. Glue to penguin head.

Use hat pattern, if desired. Cotton batting can be added to the stocking cap and/or a cotton ball used for the tip of the hat. Paper or cloth bows can also be used instead of the hat.

Insert student papers (half of an 8½ x 11 inch/21.5 x 27.5 cm paper should fit) into completed holders for display.

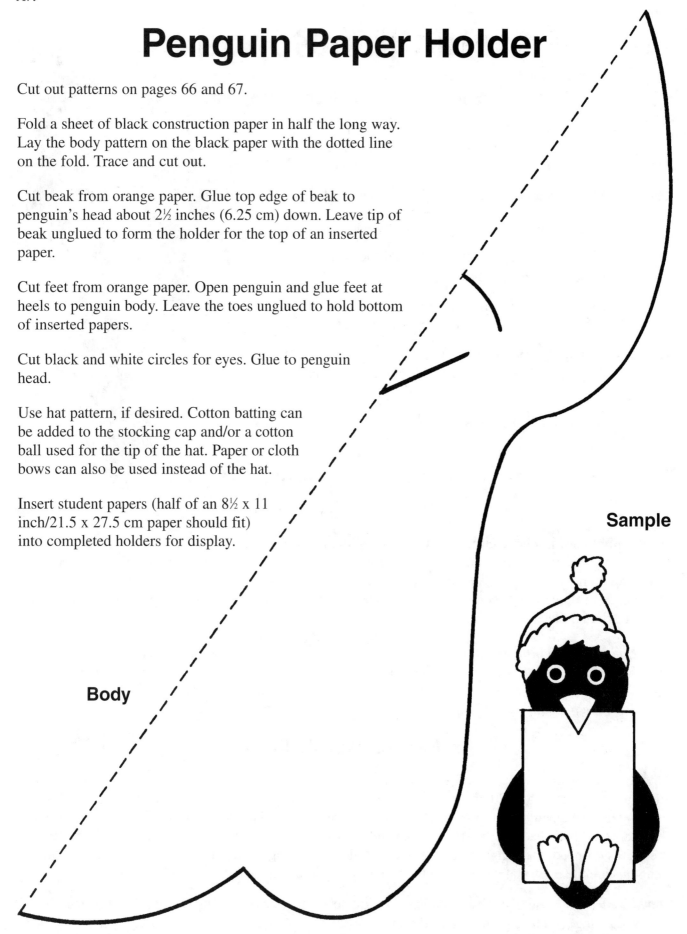

Sample

Body

Penguin Paper Holder *(cont)*

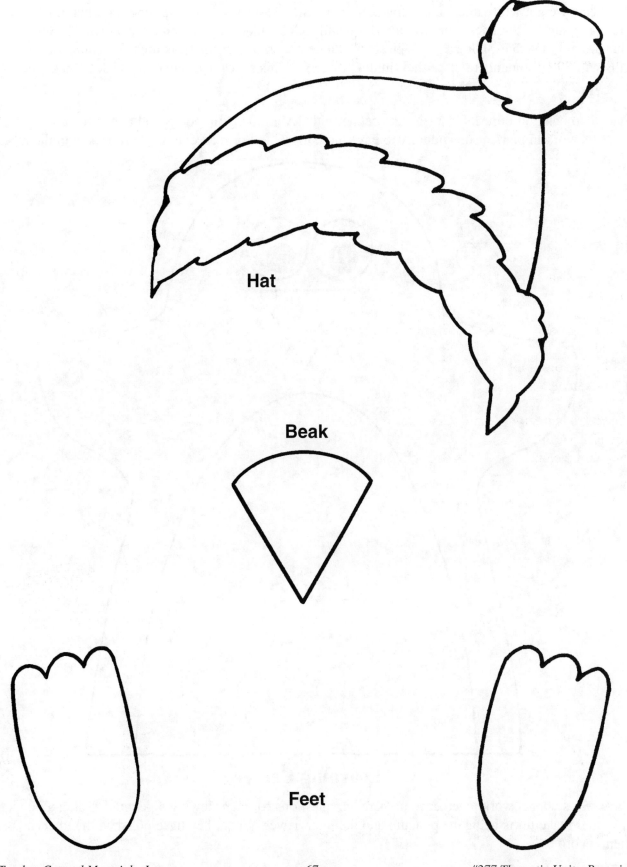

Hat

Beak

Feet

Let's Talk Penguin Puppet

Lay heavyweight white interfacing (found in fabric stores) over this basic puppet mitt pattern and trace. Trace it again for the back, omitting interior details. Color black areas with a black marker. Sew or glue around the edges. Glue a small piece of orange material over the beak area. Slit along dotted line. This will allow students to place their middle fingers in this space and move the beak to make the penguin "talk."

Place two penguin puppets in a learning center with several penguin books and a tape recorder. Let students work in pairs or individually to have the puppets tell or read one of the stories onto the tape.

Learning Center

Have two students work together to prepare ten questions for interviewing a penguin. Using a puppet, have them take turns being the penguin and the interviewer. When they have polished the interview, let them record it.

Penguin Art Activities

Frosty the Penguin

Early in the day, so that it will have time to cool, mix one cup (240 mL) Epsom salt to one cup (240 mL) boiling water. Make a construction paper penguin. (If needed, you may use the patterns on page 52, pages 66 and 67, or another favorite from this book.) Make the penguins frosty by painting over them with the Epsom salt solution using a wide brush. The penguins will have shiny "crystals" clinging to them when they dry.

Watercolor Wash

Use a sheet of white, 12" x 18" (30 x 45 cm) construction paper. Fold under 2" along the long, bottom edge. Draw and color heavily penguins, fish, and other animals that might be found in the ocean near Antarctica. Then paint over your picture with a blue watercolor wash. After the painting has dried, unfold the bottom edge and use that space to write a super sentence about your underwater painting!

Black and White All Over

Using only black and white art materials (e.g., black and white paper, crayons, chalk, paint, etc.), create a penguin in a snowy scene.

Penguin Ornaments

Mold a penguin from clay. Begin with one oval ball and three smaller, round ones. Put one of the smaller balls on top of the oval for the head. Flatten the remaining ones for flippers. Roll, flatten, and shape two smaller balls for the feet. Shape a tiny ball into a beak. Stick a paper clip into the top of the head for hanging. Let dry thoroughly. Paint and dry. Add a ribbon for hanging.

A Balanced Menu

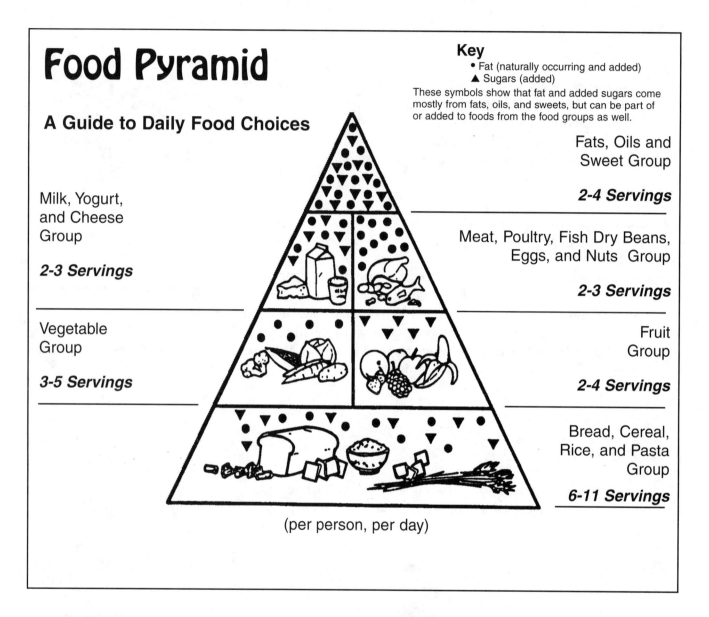

Food Pyramid

Key
• Fat (naturally occurring and added)
▲ Sugars (added)

These symbols show that fat and added sugars come mostly from fats, oils, and sweets, but can be part of or added to foods from the food groups as well.

A Guide to Daily Food Choices

Fats, Oils and Sweet Group

2-4 Servings

Milk, Yogurt, and Cheese Group

2-3 Servings

Meat, Poultry, Fish Dry Beans, Eggs, and Nuts Group

2-3 Servings

Vegetable Group

3-5 Servings

Fruit Group

2-4 Servings

Bread, Cereal, Rice, and Pasta Group

6-11 Servings

(per person, per day)

Explain to students that penguins stay healthy on a diet of just fish, but people must have a well balanced diet. Discuss the food groups represented in the diagram of the Food Pyramid. Have students give additional examples of foods in each group.

After the discussion, have students work in cooperative groups of three to plan a nutritious day of meals. Give each student a paper plate and each group some magazines to cut out pictures of food, and then glue on to the plates. By working together to plan three meals, the students will recognize that good nutrition means balanced meals throughout the day.

Feed the "Penguins"

Penguins eat only seafood. Let children make and eat some seafood treats.

Tuna Salad Spread

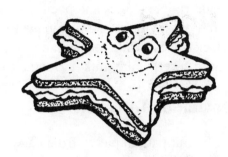

(For 2 or 3 sandwiches)
one 7 ounce (210 mL) can tuna fish
½ cup (120 mL) chopped celery
1 tablespoon (15 mL) lemon juice
¼ cup (60 mL) chopped sweet pickle
⅓ cup (80 mL) mayonnaise or salad dressing

Mix together thoroughly.

For especially fun sandwiches, cut bread into star shapes using a cookie cutter. Spread one star with tuna salad and top with a second. Use olive slices and pimento to make faces on the starfish sandwiches. They may look too cute to eat!

Shrimp Crackers

Purchase a can of wet pack shrimp. (Explain to the children that the krill eaten by penguins is similar to shrimp.) Spread a cracker with cream cheese. Place two shrimp on top. Enjoy!

Salmon Melts

Place a small amount of salmon on a shredded wheat cracker. Top with one-fourth of a slice of American cheese. Put several in a circle on a paper plate. Microwave just until cheese begins to melt. Yum!

Making Ice Cream

Make ice cream in a can. You will need the following items:

large mixer bowl
electric hand mixer (optional)
six 3 lb. (1.35 kg) coffee cans
six 1 lb. (.45 kg) coffee cans
lots of crushed ice
box of rock or table salt

6 eggs
2½ cups (625 mL) sugar
1 tablespoon (15 mL) salt
3 tablespoons (45 mL) vanilla
18 cups (4.5 L) milk

1. Beat the eggs until creamy.
2. Beat in sugar, salt, and vanilla.
3. Add the milk, 1 cup at a time.
4. Divide this mixture among the small cans.
5. Put the tops on the small cans securely; tape if necessary.

Set the small cans inside the large cans. Fill the space between the cans with layers of ice, sprinkled heavily with salt. Place the tops on the large cans securely. Give each can to a group of students. Place an old rug on the floor and have students take turns rolling the cans back and forth to each other for 20 to 30 minutes. The ice cream should be frozen and ready to eat. Be careful not to get salt water into it when removing the lids! (Note: Prepared mix may also be purchased at an ice cream store.)

Black and White Day

Have a Black and White Day in your classroom. Wear black and white clothing. Invite parents or another classroom to join you for part of the day for a Penguin Performance. Give a Readers' Theater, read original stories and poems, sing some penguin songs, and share projects completed during the unit. Send out invitations. Ask parents to send black and white snacks - black jelly beans, black licorice, black olives, white marshmallows, chocolate sandwich cookies, vanilla or chocolate chip ice cream, cauliflower, white milk—to serve for refreshments.

Invitation Directions

1. Cut pattern pieces from pages 72 and 73.

2. Trace and cut penguin body and flippers from black construction paper; penguin tummy from white paper; and feet and beak from orange paper. Use hole reinforcers for eyes.

3. Assemble penguin according to diagram. Flippers may be glued on or attached with paper fasteners.

4. Write the invitation message on the white tummy.

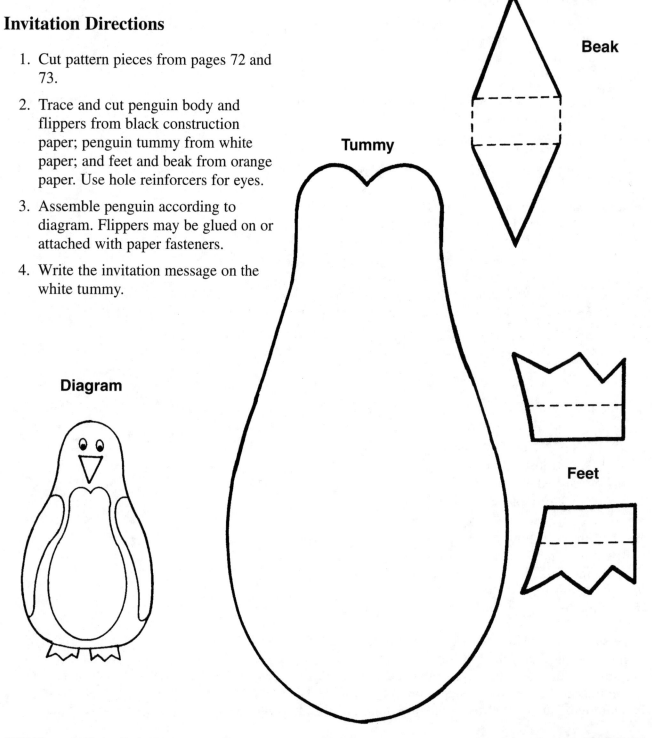

Beak

Tummy

Diagram

Feet

Black and White Day *(cont)*

Left Flipper　　　　　　　　　　　**Right Flipper**

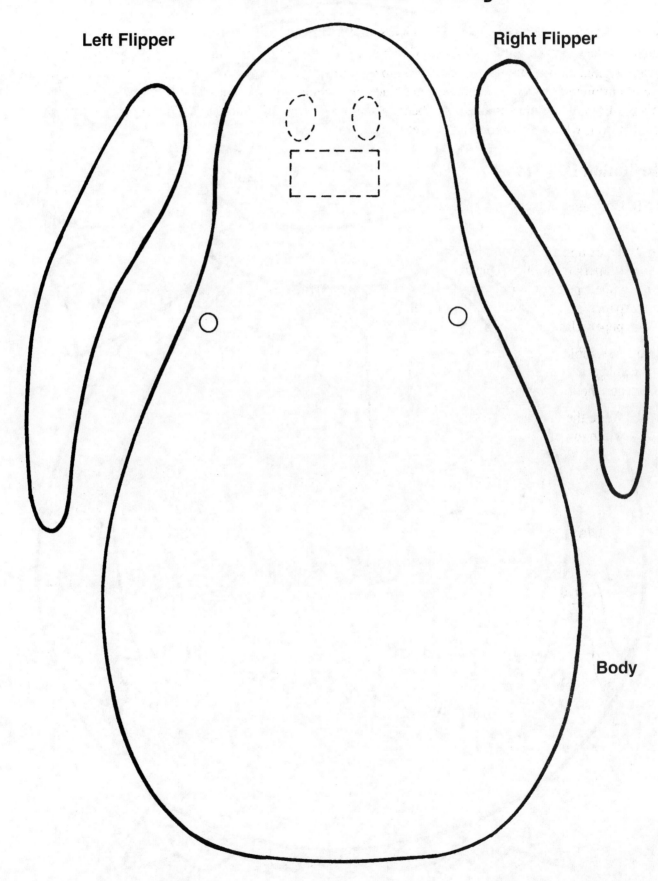

Body

Penguin Stationary

Cut around outside edge of bookmark. Cut along dotted lines so flippers flip over the top of the page.

Award and Bookmark

Award-O Grams

Cut on wave line and fold up on dotted line.

Learning Center Record

Post one of these at each learning center. Have students sign their names and put the date inside a square upon completion of the assigned learning center.

Title of Learning Center

Record Keeping

Anecdotal Records

KEY

V – vocabulary

W – written work

G – group work

M – math

A – artwork

L – language expression

0 – oral reading

S – science concepts

SS – social studies

P – physical rhythm

Using 4 x 6 inch (10 x 15 cm) index cards and a sheet of oaktag the size of this paper, create an anecdotal record for use during the penguin unit.

Tape the first index card to the oaktag 1/2 inch from the top. Title this top card as shown. Flip the card up and leaving a ¼" space, tape the next card under the first. Flip up the second card and tape as above. Continue in this manner until you have a card for each pupil. There should be ¼" exposed at the bottom of each card. Use this ¼" space to write the students' names. Clip this chart to a clipboard, use the above key or create one of your own, and keep the clipboard easily accessible. When the unit is completed, the cards can be removed and filed in children's folders for conferencing.

Four-Pocket Portfolios

Four-pocket folders can be used for organizing each child's penguin unit papers. The pockets can be labeled and illustrated: Calendar, Daily Writing, Assigned Papers, and Things I Have Learned.

These portfolios are easily made with two 12 x 18 inch (30 x 45 cm) sheets of oaktag for each folder. Fold one sheet lengthwise (hot dog fold) and one width-wise (hamburger fold). Fold the hot-dog-folded sheet up over the long bottom edge of the **open** hamburger sheet. Staple pockets with a long-armed stapler at center fold and along edges. Closed folder will have two pockets on the outside and two pockets on the inside.

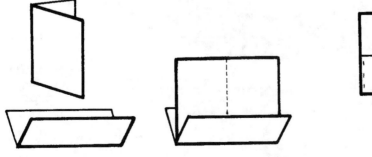

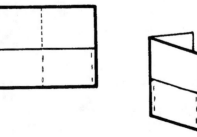

Bibliography

Fiction

Atwater, Richard and Florence. *Mr. Popper's Penguins*. Dell, 1986

Benson, Patrick. *Little Penguin*. Philomel, 1990

Brenner, Barbara. *The Penguin That Hated the Cold*. Random House, 1973

Brown, Margaret Wise. *The Important Book*. Harper and Row, 1949

Fatio, Louise. *Hector and Christina*. McGrawHill, 1977

Freeman, Don. *Penguins of All People*. Viking, 1971

Keats, Ezra Jack, *A Snowy Day*. Viking Press, 1966

Lester, Helen. *Tacky the Penguin*. Houghton Mifflin, 1988

McEwan, Chris. *The Little Penguin*. Bantam, 1988

O'Neill, Mary. *Hailstones and Halibut Bones*. Doubleday, 1961

Pfister, Marcus. *Penguin Pete*. North-South Books, 1987

Pfister, Marcus. *Penguin Pete and Pat*. North-South Books, 1989

Pfister, Marcus. *Penguin Pete's New Friends*. North-South Books, 1988

Tripp, Valerie. *The Penguin's Paint*. Children's Press, 1987

Wilhelm, Hans. *Don't Give Up, Josephine!* Random House, 1985

Winteringham, Victoria. *Penguin Day*. Harper and Row, 1982

Wood, Audrey. *Little Penguin's Tale*. HBJ, 1989

Nonfiction

Arnold, Caroline. *Penguin* (photo essay). Morrow Junior, 1988

Carle, Eric. *Animals, Animals*. Philomel, 1989

Cowcher, Helen. *Antarctica*. Farrar, Straus & Giroux, 1990

Crow, Sandra Lee. *Penguins and Polar Bears*. National Geographic, 1985

Fontanel, Beatrice. *The Penguin*. Charlesbridge, 1992

Garelick, May. *What Makes a Bird a Bird?* Follet, 1969

Heller, Ruth. *A Cache of Jewels*. Grosset & Dunlap, 1987

Johnson, Sylvia. *Penguin's Way*. Lerner, 1981 (Outstanding Science Trade Book)

Johnston, Johanna. *Penguin's Way*. Doubleday, 1962

Lepthien, Emile. *Penguins*. Childrens Press, 1983

Royston, Angela. *The Penguin*. Watts, 1988

Serventy, Vincent. *Penguin* (Animals in the Wild). Raintree, 1990

Big Books

Heller, Ruth. *Chicken's Aren't the Only Ones*. Scholastic

Nelson, Joanne. *Hatched From an Egg*. Modem Curriculum Press

Filmstrip

Fins, Feathers, Fur: Animal Groups. National Geographic

Answer Key

p. 16

From top to bottom, pictures should be numbered 2, 3, 1.

p. 30

1. $600
2. $5.00
3. $11.24
4. $80.01

p. 31

Seattle, Washington
Minneapolis, Minnesota
Milwaukee, Wisconsin
Chicago, Illinois
Detroit, Michigan
Cleveland, Ohio
Philadelphia, Pennsylvania
New York New York

p. 43

flip-slip
ice-nice
snow-show
fish-wish
black-snack

p. 45

1. stones-rocks
2. flippers-wings
3. Antarctica-South Pole
4. chilly-cool
5. protect-guard
6. fish-krill
7. sea-ocean
8. tale-story

p. 47

Penguin in lower right corner

p. 54

Larger – 3, 6, 8, 10, 13, 17, 18, 20
Smaller – 1, 2, 4, 5, 9, 11, 12, 14, 15, 16, 19

P. 55

parakeet
parrot
partridge
peacock
pelican
penguin
pheasant
pigeon

p. 56

1. false
2. true
3. false
4. true
5. true
6. true
7. false
8. true

p. 60

Amundsen
South
Scott
explorer
dogs
horses
December
January
sled
month
froze
supply
scientific
Station